Better in Black and White

Simple lessons to help photographers achieve quality monochrome prints

Harry Fearn ARPS

A CREATIVE MONOCHROME PUBLICATION

BETTER IN BLACK AND WHITE
Simple lessons to help photographers achieve quality monochrome prints
HARRY FEARN ARPS

Published in the UK by Creative Monochrome Ltd
Courtney House, 62 Jarvis Road, South Croydon, CR2 6HU

British Library Cataloguing-in-Publication Data:
A catalogue record for this book is available from the British Library

ISBN 1 873319 30 4
First edition, 2000

Printed in England by Thanet Press Limited
Union Crescent, Margate, Kent, CT9 1NU

Contents

		Page
	Introduction	5
Lesson 1:	The Zone System and tonal ranges	7
Lesson 2:	Exposure, development and negative density	13
Lesson 3:	Film development	23
Lesson 4:	Basics of printing	30
Lesson 5:	Printing technique	37
Lesson 6:	Refining printing control	44
Lesson 7:	Presenting your image	48
Lesson 8:	Examples	53
	Index	63

WARNING

This book explains the Ansel Adams 'Zone System' method of working, which may seriously improve your photography. Good photography can be addictive, leading to huge expenditure of time and money.

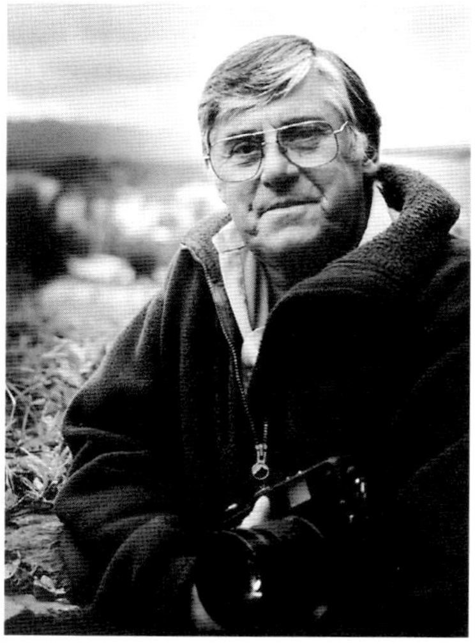

HARRY FEARN is a qualified adult education tutor, who lives and works in Porthmadog, North Wales. From this base, his fine art photography has gained widespread national recognition. He is the author of *Improve your photography overnight*, which was a bestseller.

Harry's work has been exhibited at various locations around the UK and he has lectured at numerous prestigious venues, including the National Museum of Photography, Film and Television in Bradford, Yorkshire. He has, until recently, regularly tutored photographic workshops for members of The Royal Photographic Society at its headquarters in Bath.

As a child, Harry recalls looking longingly at the Ilford Sportsman camera in the window of the local chemist's shop, such was his desire to make photographs. That passion has never left him, although his enthusiasm faltered after years of working with colour negative film. He was on the point of selling his camera gear when a friend suggested he should first try monochrome. "Wham! The impact was immediate; I became totally hooked on the medium."

It was then that the problems began. Harry just couldn't get his prints to match the standards of the 'great' monochrome photographers he had seen in books and magazines."I honestly thought they had some kind of magic that I was unaware of. They did, of course: it's called 'technique'. Their 'secret' was in understanding how all the elements came together."

Harry set about learning these secrets and has spent a good deal of his time subsequently in sharing these pearls with others. He describes himself as "a very simple man" – and this has gifted him the ability to express quite complex technical ideas in terms which others can readily assimilate. Photographically, he is a 'free spirit', turning his camera to a wide range of varied subjects.

Harry has a particular admiration for photographers who impart great emotion through their work. "My inspiration comes from work that displays depth, warmth and intimacy. I am drawn to photographers who are capable of introducing 'feel' into their work. Maybe, at the end of the day, I'm just an incurable romantic."

Introduction

Photography should be a simple and enjoyable activity. And yet many people come to my photographic workshops after years of struggle and frustration, still searching for the elixir of photographic life.

Many of these photographers, as their images consistently fail to capture the potential of the original scene, have progressed from one supposed magic formula to another: a new camera or lens; a new film or developer (or combination of the two); a new printing paper. This search, naturally encouraged by the manufacturers of photographic equipment and materials, misses a key point. These items are all tools, and tools (as all good workmen will tell you) are of little help unless you know how to use them.

Technique is the answer. Master technique and your artistic ability will be free to flourish.

One of the great personal pleasures derived from my workshops is to see the photographic 'penny' drop and to witness the transformation in students' work as they learn to apply some simple lessons. Suddenly they have negatives that are a pleasure to print and the images begin to fulfil what was seen at the time of making the exposure. It is as if a huge weight has been taken off their photographic shoulders. This sense of freedom is precisely what I hope to achieve through the pages of this book.

But 'technique' does not mean 'complex'. Several people have told me that my forte is my ability to convey information very simply. If that is so, then I am pleased, because for me simplicity of approach is of paramount importance. I am firmly committed to simplicity because I know it works. Mastering technique in its most basic form is very necessary, it does matter. Good technique enables photographers to have total control over their work, from the taking stage through to the finished print. This mastery means that the photographer can visualise how the final print will appear before firing the camera shutter. Once logical and proven methods of working have been understood and mastered, the photographer is set free to concentrate solely on subject matter and composition.

Several years ago I wrote and published a booklet entitled *Improve Your Photography Overnight*, in which I tried to encapsulate as briefly as possible the basic tenets of sound monochrome technique. A few thousand negatives later, the tremendous response to that booklet and the requests from many readers and workshop students have encouraged me to expand a little on those ideas in this book. I have taken the opportunity to stand back and look at what I have done photographically over that period and to try to recall those ideas which seem to have offered most help to other photographers who have looked to me for advice.

I have structured this book on the basis of the lesson plans that I have prepared as the basis for my teaching over several years. I hope readers will find this a useful method for explaining the basics simply and concisely. I did not want to produce a technical book – there are dozens of these, and from the feedback I have received, not too many people appear to understand them. My belief is that many photographers acquire such books like good luck charms – hoping that having the latest technical tome unread on their bookshelf will, by some process of osmosis, conjure superb images from their cameras and darkrooms. The evidence suggests overwhelmingly that this does not work!

What I have tried to produce here is a book explaining how all the elements of good photography come together and interact: a practical book of simple logic that people can readily assimilate and put into practice.

As I say at the outset of any workshop, it is unlikely that I shall be telling anyone anything that they do not already know. But I hope that the simple explanations I offer will act as the catalyst to crystallise your thinking, to channel the thought processes so that the different parts of the jig-saw click into place.

I would like to dedicate this book to my super family and to the people and acquaintances that I have met through my interest in photography, some of whom have become truly wonderful and valued friends.

LESSON 1

The Zone System and tonal ranges

This lesson covers:

- The Zone System
- The tonal range of a scene or subject
- The tonal scale
- Pre-visualisation (or, according to preference, 'visualisation')
- The photographic process in its most basic form.

In order to work towards a high level of consistency in our photographic work, we have to:

a) devise a methodical system of working;

b) fully understand how all the elements work together from the taking of the photograph through to the final print presentation.

The famous American photographer Ansel Adams devised a systematic method of working which met the above criteria. He named this as the 'Zone System' and used it to produce his superb, world famous monochrome prints.

Adams determined that a photographic scene or subject with a full range of tones from the blackest black through to the whitest white could, for practical purposes, be divided into a series of ten tones or zones (see Figure 1). In reality, of course there is a continuous and almost immeasurable range of tones between black and white: you will see later that simplifying this continuous range into ten zones is a practical way of identifying the important areas of an image as the basis for determining correct exposure. All will become clear as we progress!

PRE-VISUALISATION

It can be helpful to think of the Zone System as a visual slide rule which one uses and considers to make certain decisions. As our experience and confidence grows, we can look at a scene or subject and determine exactly how we would like this image to appear in the final print. For example, we can decide how dark we want the shadows to appear or how bright the highlights should be. This is known as **pre-visualisation**. Having pictured the final print in our mind's eye, we

Figure 1: In the Zone System the continuous range of tones from black to white is simplified to ten distinct zones, depicted by convention using Roman numerals

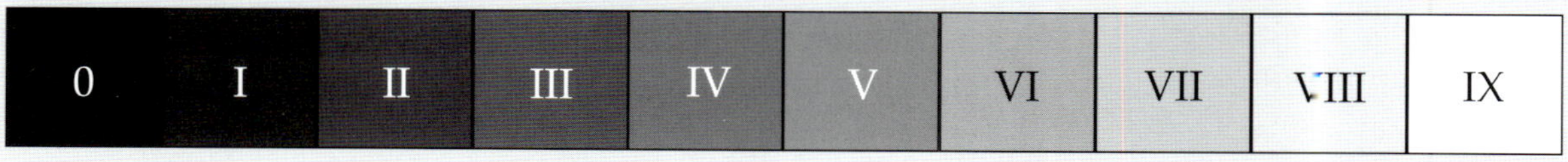

can then make our decisions on exposure. Pre-visualisation enables us to identify tones or zones. Once we have identified these tones, we can move up or down the scale of the slide rule accordingly when taking our exposure meter readings and ultimately determining our camera settings. By using a set method of working with our film, developers and ultimately through to the printing paper, we can determine how our final print will appear *before* firing the camera shutter.

If the thought of visual slide rules and the sight of Roman numerals is already making you nervous, don't worry! Just fix your sights on the purpose: to be able to produce in the print what you had in mind when you took the picture.

ADVANTAGES OF THE ZONE SYSTEM

There are numerous advantages of using the Zone System, but the primary ones can be summarised as:

Establishing a consistent approach
Consistency means that we can replicate results: we know what to expect if we adopt procedures that we have tried and tested.

Developing a fuller understanding of the photographic process
Using the Zone System, we gain a better understanding of what happens when film is exposed to light and then processed. This enables us to take control of our photography.

Analysing and assessing our work
All photographers come up against the image which "does not come out" as expected. The important thing in this event is to be able to work out what has gone wrong, so that under similar circumstances in future, the same mistakes can be avoided.

Gaining a higher level of photographic awareness and confidence
Once we are aware of our ability to control the elements contained in a photograph, we then begin to look at light differently. When that happens, we start to 'see' differently. We can look at what we are photographing in a more subjective and confident manner, fully aware that what we see at the taking stage will be reproduced in the final print.

Before we can really start to understand how to take control of our photography, it will help to know what happens in the process of making a photograph. Please don't skip the following section: it will help you later!

THE PHOTOGRAPHIC PROCESS

Few technical books on photography cover the photographic process in its most basic form, but understanding these basics is the key to why the Zone System works and therefore also the key to improving your photography.

The film

Film is produced from a clear piece of celluloid or acetate. This is coated with a chemical emulsion, the main ingredient being **silver halides** (millions of them per square centimetre), which are sensitive to light.

Exposure

When the film is exposed to light via the camera, the silver halides react by gathering and retaining light. Obviously, they gather and retain more light from a highlight area (the brightest part of the subject) than from a shadow area (the darkest part of a subject), with all the varying degrees of light in between recording as different densities.

When a film has been exposed to light, but before being developed, the 'image' is held dormant on the film. This is referred to as the **'latent image'**.

Processing

When the film is developed, the silver halides which have been exposed to light expand and become denser and therefore more opaque. In a totally white area of the scene, the silver halides will reach a maximum density. Think of the developer as food for the halides: the ones that have 'seen' more light try to take on the most developer and thus expand to form clumps.

After development, the film is 'fixed' in chemicals which make the film no longer sensitive to light. At this stage, the silver halides which did not record any light are rendered useless and are subsequently washed away with the fix. This leaves the film (which has now become the negative) clear or translucent in what were the very darkest areas of the original scene.

Note: The clearest part of the negative will still have some evidence of chemicals. This area is referred to as **'film base + fog'**.

Negative density

When you look at your negative after processing, you will see that the area of the negative that contains the shadow area from the original scene is 'thin' or translucent, whereas the highlights of the original scene are now relatively opaque. If you could turn the negative on its side and view it through a microscope, you would find that the negative was literally 'thinner' where the subject shadow area was and 'thicker' in the area of the original highlight.

Imagine that we had photographed a zone scale as depicted in the lower half of figure 1, and then turned the negative on its side and viewed it through a microscope. The density ('thickness') of the negative would register as a series of steps, with the thinnest section being the darkest shadow area (Zone 0 = film base + fog) and the thickest being the brightest highlight area (Zone IX). We can map these density steps out on a bar chart (shown in figure 2). If we performed the same exercise for the continous tone scale in figure 1, we could chart the density from Zone 0 to Zone IX as a continuous line on a graph. This line is known as the **characteristic curve** for the film. (For simplicity, we have shown the characteristic curve as a straight line between Zone 0 and Zone IX; in reality, the relationship is

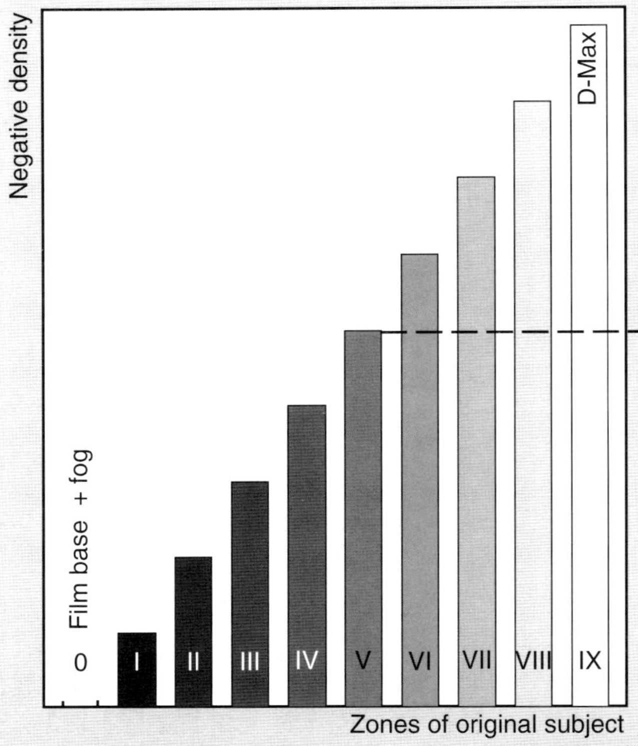

Figure 2: The density (or 'thickness') of the negative is greater, the brighter is the area of the original subject. So, for example, shadow areas will be relatively 'thin' and highlights relatively dense.

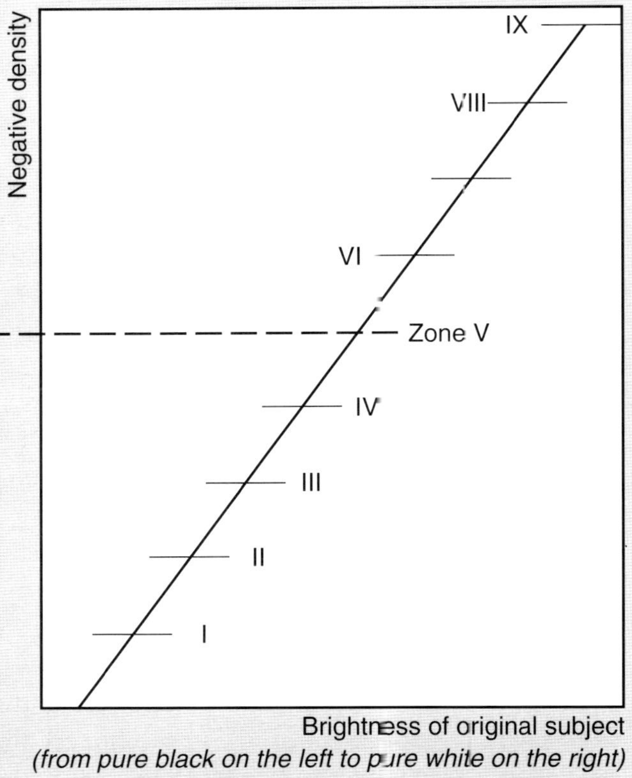

Figure 3: Joining the mid-points at the top of each bar in Figure 2 produces the 'characteristic curve', showing the negative density for a continuous range of tones from black to white.

a little more complex. For the time being, understanding the principle is the key.)

The next stage of the photographic process is to make a print from the negative. Printing paper is simply a sheet of paper which has been coated with light-sensitive chemicals. The paper is normally white and it is this whiteness (referred to as **paper base white**) which controls and determines the maximum whiteness in our final print. However, you only need to compare sheets of white paper from different sources (such as this book, a newspaper and a sheet of writing paper) to see that different papers have different base whites. You cannot print any whiter than the paper base white of the paper you choose.

The tones achieved when printing from a negative depend on the amount of

Having trouble understanding the graphs?

The charts and graphs are intended as a simple way to picture an idea or principle. However, I know that some people have a mental block as soon as a graph appears. If you find the above charts difficult, don't panic! All you need to understand is that the more light that reaches the film, the thicker (and therefore less translucent) is the negative.

If you photograph the proverbial black cat in the cellar, the negative will appear clear ('thin'); if you shoot a piece of white paper reflecting sunlight, the negative will appear opaque ('thick'). These two extremes are, respectively, known as film base + fog and D-Max (or maximum density). In between the two extremes, the negative gets more dense (and therefore less translucent) the more light reaches the film.

light reaching the light-sensitive paper: the more light, the darker the printed tone will be.

If we were to make a print from our Figure 2 negative, we would find that the area of the negative which was translucent (ie film base – fog) would print to detail-less black ('max black') in the final print. This is because there is nothing blocking the light being transmitted from the enlarger lamp. Conversely, the area where the negative was most dense 'prints' as paper base white. This is because the enlarger lamp cannot transmit light through this opaque part of the film. As shown in Figure 4, for a given amount of exposure to the enlarger light, progressively less light reaches the paper as the negative density increases, causing the corresponding printed tones to become lighter. What the printing process is doing is to convert the varying densities of the negative back to the corresponding brightness of the original scene or subject.

So the principle of the photographic process is very simple. The brightness of the original scene determines the density of the negative, and the density of the negative determines the brightness of the tones in the print. Obvious, isn't it?

Photographers who find it difficult to produce quality prints have generally lost sight of how simple the photographic process is. For some reason, they have sought to make it more complicated. If you remember the key points from this first lesson, you will be able to analyse your results quickly and easily and will be able to take any necessary remedial actions to rectify faults.

If it is all that simple, why can't everyone make perfect prints every time? The answer lies in exposure and development, which is what we will consider in more detail in the next lesson.

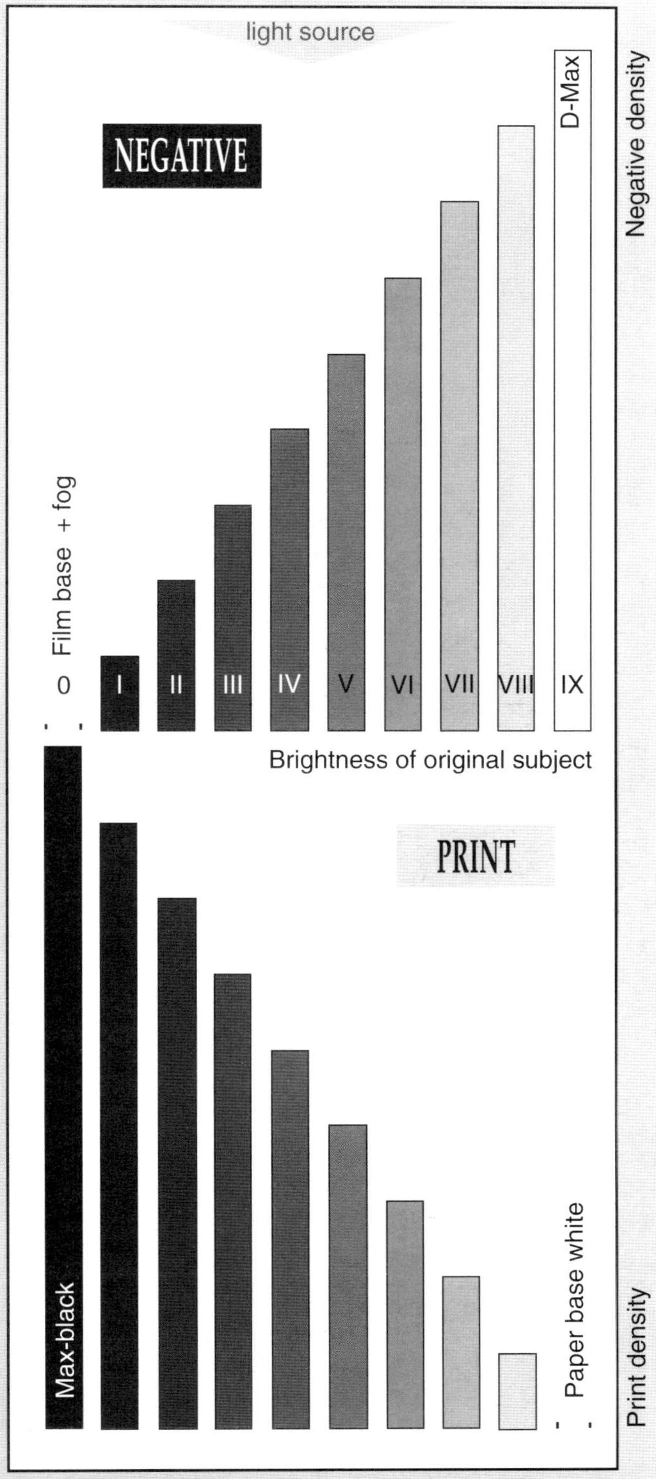

Figure 4: The density of the print depends on how much of the light from the enlarger is allowed to pass through the negative to reach the light-sensitive printing paper. When the negative is printed, the 'thin' areas allow more light to pass through, making the print darker. Conversely, the denser areas of the negative restrict the amount of light reaching the paper and therefore appear lighter in the print. At the extremes, the D-Max area of a negative will prevent any light reaching the paper, leaving paper base white in the print, whilst the film base + fog part of the negative will print as max-black (ie without any detail of the original scene showing through).

Summary of Lesson 1

The **Zone System** is basically a visual slide rule which enables us to look at a subject and **pre-visualise** the tones of the print we want to make of it.

The Zone System simplifies the **range of tones** in a scene or subject to ten distinct zones, from black (Zone 0) to white (Zone IX). Of course, not all subjects will contain the full range of tones.

Photographic film is coated with **silver halides** which are sensitive to light. When the film is exposed, the silver halides retain the light in the **latent image** until the film is developed. During development, the silver halides which have been exposed to light expand, making the negative denser and less transluscent.

The densest areas of the negative are those which were subjected to most light. At the extremes, bright white is the most opaque (densest) area of the negative, known as **D-Max**, whilst featureless black is the thinnest part of the negative, known as **film base + fog**. The **characteristic curve** of the film shows how the amount of light reaching the film from the subject corresponds to the density of the negative.

When printing, the more light that is able to pass through an area of a negative, the darker the corresponding tone of the print. Thus, the more dense areas of the negative print as light tones, whereas the 'thinner' parts of the negative print darker. At the extremes, film base + fog prints as **Max black**, whilst D-Max prevents light reaching the paper, leaving it as **paper base white**.

The key principle of the photographic process is beautifully simple: the brightness of the original scene determines the density of the negative, and the density of the negative determines the brightness of the tones in the print.

LESSON 2

Exposure, development and negative density

This lesson covers:

- Correct exposure
- How to measure the tonal range of a scene or subject
- How to determine correct development times.

FILM SPEEDS

Every film has a given speed, which is basically the time it takes the film to react to light. There are slow, medium and fast speeds of film, denoted by the manufacturer's ISO (or ASA) rating. The ISO rating is simply a standard for measurement of the sensitivity of film to light: the lower the number, the slower the speed of the film. To achieve the correct exposure for a given subject, a slow film will require more exposure than a fast film.

The choice of film speed depends on the combination of three main factors:

Grain

The crystal structure of the silver halides on the negative surface produces a pattern known as 'grain'. Slow films have very fine grain which is barely noticeable in the print, whereas faster films have coarser grain which can readily be seen even at relatively small enlargements. The degree to which noticeable grain is acceptable in the finished print will therefore be a significant influence on choice of film speed. For many photographers, fine print quality is synonymous with absence of noticeable grain.

Available light

Because slow films need more light to achieve the correct exposure, there will be circumstances when the amount of available light will dictate very slow shutter speeds. If the camera and subject are not perfectly still during such exposures, the print will be blurred. Fast films have the advantage that the camera can be hand-held in relatively dim lighting conditions.

Use of a tripod

With slow films, the risk of camera movement during relatively long exposures can be eliminated by use of a tripod and cable release (although this does not, of course, eliminate the possibility of subject movement). Using a tripod involves more effort – and more weight to carry 'in the field'

– and results in less spontaneity: for some subjects (such as landscapes), this can be an advantage (giving time for more considered composition, for example), whereas for others (such as candid people shots) it is unlikely to be a practical option. As a general rule, use a tripod unless there is a good reason not to.

Only you know what type of photography you wish to pursue and the nature of the finished result you want to achieve, so the final choice is yours. But remember, whatever speed of film is used, the principles applied are the same:

CORRECT EXPOSURE IS CORRECT EXPOSURE

There are two main types of black and white film in current use: panchromatic and dye-based. The dye-based (or 'chromogenic') films are processed in colour chemicals and therefore the development processes that we will be discussing do not apply. We will only be looking at the development of panchromatic films.

Exposure procedures are the same for all types of film. Correct exposure is correct exposure and applies to all films, be they black and white (whether panchromatic or dye-based) or colour films (whether negative or slide).

EXPOSURE INDEX

Correct exposure is determined from the Exposure Index (EI) of the chosen film and works on the basis that in order to expose the film correctly, it needs to receive a given amount of light. To allow us to set our exposure meters (be they hand held or in camera) correctly, the film manufacturer states on the film box an ISO number. This is the effective speed rating of the film and normally (though not always – more on this later) this is the setting that we would use on our meter.

THINKING IN STOPS

Before we progress to film exposure, I would like to introduce those of you who are not already familiar with them to 'stops'. We will refer to these right from exposing our film through to making the print in the darkroom, so I recommend that you get to know and understand them, and importantly, think in them.

One stop either doubles or halves the amount of light reaching the film (or, in the darkroom, the printing paper). We control the amount of light reaching the film by the combination of the camera's shutter speed selector and the lens aperture ring.

It is common to talk about 'opening up' or 'closing down' by a stop. Changing the shutter speed from 1/30 to 1/60 of a second, halves the amount of light reaching the film (closing down by one stop), whereas moving from 1/30 to 1/15 of a second, doubles the amount of light reaching the film (opening up by one stop). Think of 'closing down' as cutting down the amount of light: the phrase actually comes from controlling exposure by use of the aperture, where making the hole smaller ('closing down') cuts down the light reaching the film and making the hole bigger ('opening up') increases the light getting to the film.

The measurement of progressive stops on the aperture ring is less intuitive than for shutter speeds: we won't go into the reasons for this now, but the main f/stops on most cameras are: f/2.8, f/4, f/5.6, f/8, f/11, f/16, f/22. The smallest number is the largest aperture (literally the 'hole' through which the light passes).

Shutting down the aperture by one stop from f/5.6 to f/8 halves the amount of light reaching the film, whereas opening up by one stop from f/5.6 to f/4 doubles the amount of light reaching the film.

All the vertical combinations of shutter and aperture settings in the chart below result in the same amount of light reaching the film (the Exposure Value or 'EV'):

Shutter	1/15	1/30	1/60	1/125	1/250	1/500
Aperture	f/22	f/16	f/11	f/8	f/5.6	f/4

To close down by one stop (halve the light reaching the film), move the aperture scale one place to the right (or the shutter scale one place to the left) and read off the vertical combinations, any of which result in an equal amount of light reaching the film:

	Shutter	1/15	1/30	1/60	1/125	1/250	1/500	
Close down one stop		Aperture	f/22	f/16	f/11	f/8	f/5.6	f/4

Starting from the original Exposure Value, to open up by one stop (double the light reaching the film), move the aperture scale one place to the left (or the shutter scale one place to the right) and read off the vertical combinations:

	Shutter	1/15	1/30	1/60	1/125	1/250	1/500
Aperture	f/22	f/16	f/11	f/8	f/5.6	f/4	**Open up one stop (from the original EV)**

Figure 5: There are several combinations of shutter speeds and f/stops to achieve the same amount of light reaching the film, measured as an Exposure Value (EV).

As we saw at the beginning of the lesson, the amount of light which needs to reach the film to achieve correct exposure depends on the speed of the film: slow films needing more light than fast films. The ISO (or ASA) rating of a film also works in stops: ISO 100 is one stop faster than ISO 50 and one stop slower than ISO 200. So for a given scene, if we keep the shutter speed constant, there are several combinations of film speed and aperture to achieve the same Exposure Value, as shown below:

Film speed	ISO 800	ISO 400	ISO 200	ISO 100	ISO 50	ISO 25
Aperture	f/22	f/16	f/11	f/8	f/5.6	f/4

Similarly, we could keep the aperture constant, and chart the combinations of shutter speed and film speed which will give the same exposure value. So we have three variables in determining the correct exposure: film speed, shutter speed and the aperture. Once you have loaded the camera with a film, of course, the film speed is essentially fixed, and we vary exposure with the shutter speed and aperture settings on the camera. For a given film, your choice of which shutter speed and aperture combination to use will depend on a number of factors, such as:

• whether you are using a tripod or hand-holding the camera

• the degree of subject movement

• the range over which you want the image to appear sharp ('depth of field')

• the performance of the lens at different apertures (most lenses give a crisper rendition of a subject in the mid-range of the available apertures).

Thinking in stops helps us in moving between the available combinations of shutter speed, aperture and film speed.

Remember: 1 EV = 1 Stop = 1 Zone = 1 Tone

MEASURING THE LIGHT

In order to set the right exposure, we first have to be able to measure the light reflected from the subject we wish to photograph. The instrument used for this purpose is the **light meter**, whether built-in to the camera or a separate piece of equipment. Light meters usually display the aperture and shutter speed settings to achieve a given Exposure Value, depending on the speed of the film in use. Many meters also show the EV number itself.

In automatic cameras, it is common for the user to set either the required aperture or the required shutter speed and for the camera to adjust the other variable as appropriate to achieve the required EV. Metering systems built-in to cameras have become increasingly sophisticated, but unfortunately they cannot think: they do what they have been calibrated to do.

The standard reference point from which meters are calibrated is the Kodak **18% reflected grey card** (corresponding to Zone V on the tonal scale). This, in theory, means that no matter what exposure meter we use, provided it works correctly and has been calibrated correctly, then the same reading will be displayed when measured against the same reference point.

We must remember that the exposure meter is an instrument, it can't think. It does not know what you are measuring from. It can only measure the amount of light falling on the subject. Every time you ask it to measure how much light is falling on the subject to be photographed, it assumes that subject to be **18% grey**. If you point it in a dark cave it will assume that the cave is grey. If you point it to a bright sky it assumes that the sky is grey. It does this simply because that is what it has been designed and calibrated to do.

The vast majority of photographers go wrong at this stage because they set the camera to the readings given by the exposure meter, no matter what the meter is pointing at. This is why they obtain flat negatives which display the wrong tonal values. In using the reading displayed by the meter (unless metering from a mid grey area) they have already either under exposed or over exposed the film. This in turn makes the negative difficult to print because the amount of light trying to pass through the negative is incorrectly balanced. How can a black be achieved if insufficient light is reaching the paper? Or how can we retain paper base white if too much light is causing the paper to fog? We are already in a position where we know that we are going to struggle to produce a print. We know that we are going to start messing about dodging and burning-in to produce a mediocre image – and we haven't even started printing!

Let me explain.

Earlier I described the Zone System as "a visual slide rule". As such, we must learn visually to recognise the tones (zones) in a given scene or subject. We also know that our meter is calibrated to an 18% reflected grey card, which is the equivalent of Zone V. What we as photographers must do is learn how to interpret and use the information our exposure meter is giving us.

Our meter can reveal a large amount of information, such as the amount of light falling on the subject and, importantly, the amount of light falling on different parts of the subject. It also allows us to determine what camera settings to use, and how long we need to develop our film for. And as our experience grows, it will also tell us what paper grade we will probably need to use when printing in the darkroom – now you can see why it is referred to as pre-visualisation! All this information is readily available via our exposure meter if only we take the trouble to learn how to use it and understand what it is telling us. A hand held exposure meter is probably the most vital piece of equipment that you will ever purchase. It is even more important than the camera itself: a good photographer, using an exposure meter correctly, will turn out stunning images from the most basic of cameras.

At this stage, I would strongly recommend anyone who is thinking about photography seriously to consider buying a **spot meter**. They are not cheap, but they are wonderful instruments which will enable you to measure all around the subject to be photographed and determine exactly where all the tonal values will lie on the negative.

Let's look at how to use our meters correctly.

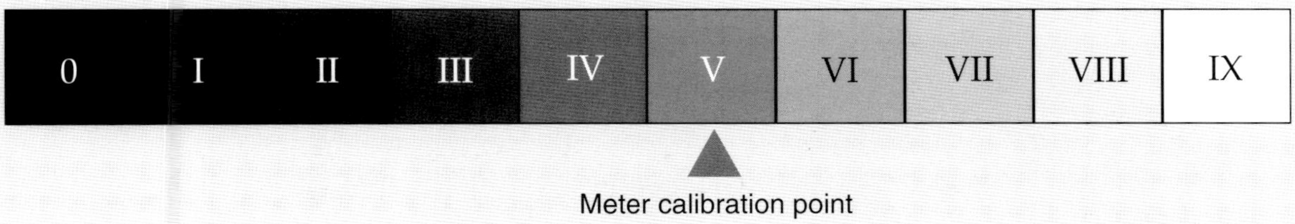

As we can see, the meter calibration point is exactly in the middle of the tonal scale. Were we to meter from nothing but mid-greys, our readings would always be correct; but unfortunately nothing is as simple as that, and we therefore have to learn to understand what our meter is telling us and then translate this into a practical application.

It may seem difficult to break down and identify the tones on the tonal scale and our personal interpretation of these right through the ten tones. This is not as difficult as it first appears because the tonal scale represents various tonalities and textures in the subject to be photographed. We only need to concern ourselves with the fully textured zones.

A good print represents three types of Zones (tones); these break down as follows:

a) No texture, extremely dark or pure white (Zones O, I and IX)

b) Almost none or very limited texture (Zones II, and VIII)

c) Full texture and detail. These make up the greatest part of the photograph (Zones III, IV, V, VI, VII)

Let's just review the tonal values which each of the Zones represent:

ZONES	TONAL VALUES
O & I	The deepest black shadow areas
II	Shadow areas with *just discernible* detail showing
III, IV, V, VI & VII	The fully textured areas in the photograph
VIII	Highlight areas with *just discernible* detail showing
IX	The whitest white we are able to produce (paper base white)

It is not to difficult to break these areas down because we can do very little about Zones O, 1 & II in the deep shadow areas and also Zones VIII and IX in the very bright highlight areas. Generally speaking, these Zones are too difficult to ascertain and meter from. For the time being, therefore, let's be aware that they exist and that we may want to reproduce them in our prints, but forget them when taking exposure meter readings. (Ignoring these Zones for metering purposes doesn't mean that we will lose deep shadows or bright highlights in the print, as will become clear later.)

So, we are left with Zones III, IV, V, VI & VII for metering purposes. These five Zones are the most important zones. They are the fully textured zones. *Always use these zones to meter from.* I refer to them as the 'Five Golden Zones'.

There is an old adage in photography which says:

EXPOSE for the SHADOWS
DEVELOP for the HIGHLIGHTS

Get to grips with this simple proposition, and you won't go far wrong.

So how do we interpret what we are seeing and how do we adjust or set our camera accordingly? Let's imagine that we are photographing a subject which contains a full range of tones. This is what we need to do:

1) Look for a Zone III (fully textured shadow area).

TIP: Look for a shadow area in which you can see detail; then screw up your eyes (the equivalent of closing down your eyes by two stops) – if the detail disappears, you have Zone II; if you can still see detail with your eyes screwed up, you are looking at the higher value Zone III.

2) Take a meter reading from this Zone III area.

3) Transfer this reading onto your camera (but DON'T fire the shutter).

4) Close down the aperture by two stops.
   (eg If the meter reading gave an aperture of f/8 at a given speed, set the aperture at f/16 at the same speed – remember, the higher the f-stop, the smaller the lens aperture.)

5) Now you can fire your camera shutter.

What we have done, in fact, is to reduce the exposure indicated by the meter in order to make our negative 'thinner' (ie more translucent) in the shadow areas. (Remember that the exposure meter is calibrated to tell us the exposure required to achieve Zone V, so having metered a Zone III area, it is logical to close down the camera by two stops to make it record as Zone III rather than Zone V.) By doing this, we will benefit at the printing stage because we shall be allowing the light from our enlarger to have an easy passage through this portion of the negative onto our printing paper, thereby printing accordingly darker.

Note: Some people state that you should under-expose for the shadow areas. I would urge you not to think in this manner because you are not under-exposing. What you are in fact doing is giving the film the correct amount of exposure for the shadows areas.

Talking about exposure in the abstract, can make it seem a lot more complex than it is, so let's look at the practical example in figure 8 (page 20). The fully textured shadow area of the scene was placed on Zone III – that gave me the metered reading, from which I closed down by two stops.

I then measured the contrast range of the scene and found that the fully textured highlight area that I wished to display (the strongest highlight on the fence) then fell onto Zone VII. This five f/stop range between Zone III and Zone VII was just about right. The white areas of cloud fell on Zone VIII and the other areas of the fence fell on a high Zone VI. No filters were used. The film was given Normal (N) development.

By reading from the textured shadow area and then closing down by two stops, I had set all the fully textured areas within the five f-stop range of the film. If we gave less exposure, we would lose the detail in the shadow areas. If we gave more exposure, the increased density of the film would make the highlights more difficult to print and would increase the graininess of the print.

Of course, not all scenes cover the five fully textured zones, although in practice you may be surprised how often they do. Under some circumstances, it may be necessary to meter from the highlights. In a snow scene, for example, it may be necessary to meter from Zone VIII (the brightest highlight in which you can discern detail without screwing up your eyes). Remembering that the meter is calibrated to give the exposure for rendering at Zone V whatever it is pointed at, this reading would render the white snow as mid-grey on the negative, so it is necessary to open up by three stops in this case. This will ensure that the highlight detail is recorded without the negative becoming so dense that it is difficult to print and grainy. (Shadow detail below Zone IV would be lost if, when measured, the tonal range of the scene did not display a 5-6 stop range.)

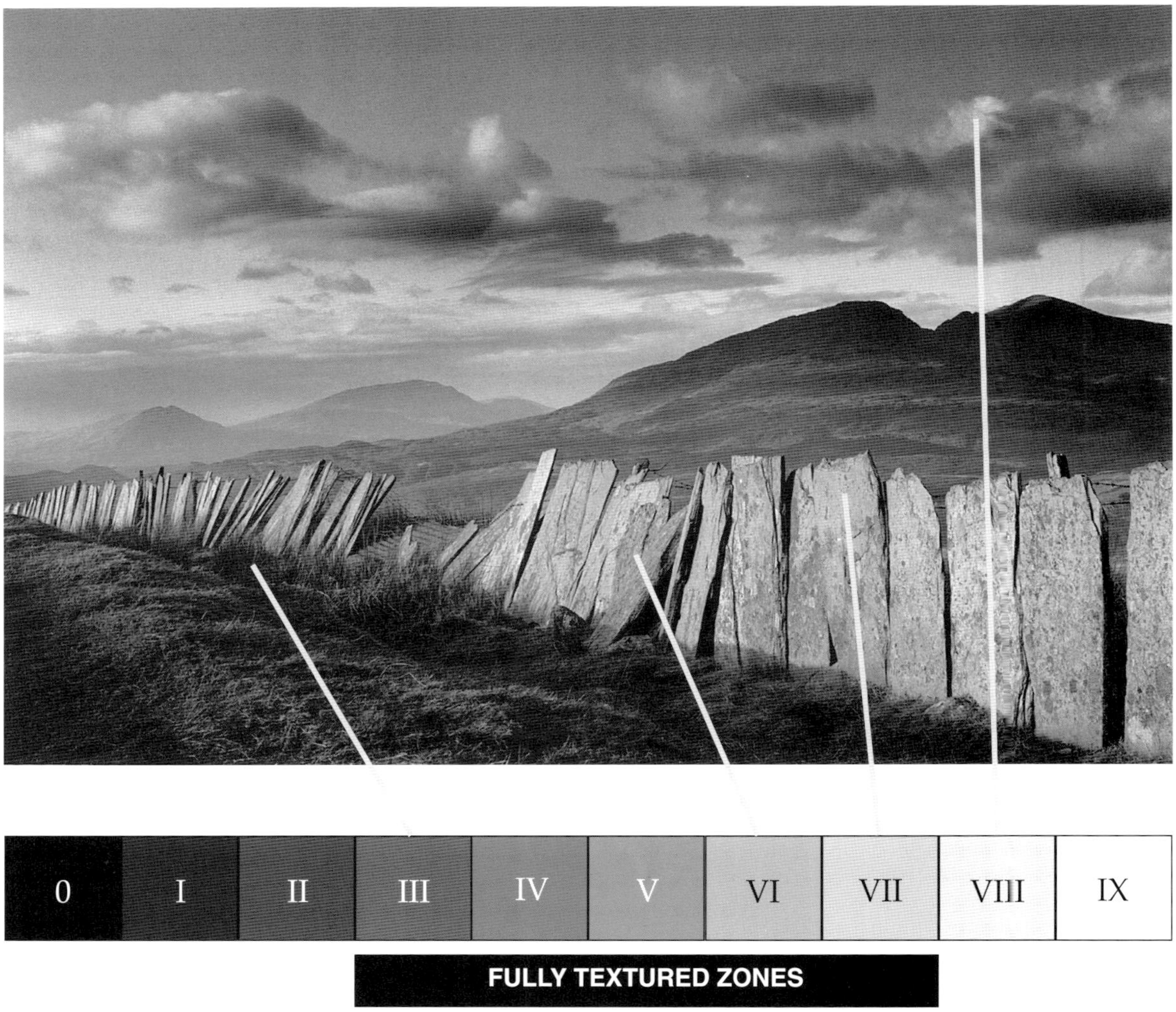

Figure 8– 'Reading' the tonal values of a scene

One way of visualising the exposure judgement is to imagine your film as a block covering five zones (see figure 9). Take your meter reading from the zone at whichever end of the block is the most convenient. If you chose the shadow end of the block (which is generally recommended), close down by two stops from the exposure reading for that area; if you choose the highlight end of the block, open up by two stops.

Where the tonal range is greater or less than five stops, you can compensate for this by adjusting the normal ('N') development time. If the tonal range is less than a five-stop block, you can use extended ('N+') development to increase the contrast range; if it is more than five stops, you can use reduced ('N-') development to decrease the contrast and give a wider tonal range. These techniques are explained in detail in the next 'lesson'.

We can meter from any of the five textured Zones as long as we remember to close down or open up accordingly. But, in my opinion, if you wish to strive for absolute perfection, always aim to meter from the Zone III shadow area. That is certainly the way to meter if you are using individual sheet film, when you can control the development times for each individual negative (more about that later when we discuss development times); but sometimes when using roll film we have to compromise and that may mean selecting the most important part of the image, determining on which Zone we wish to place that area and then adjusting

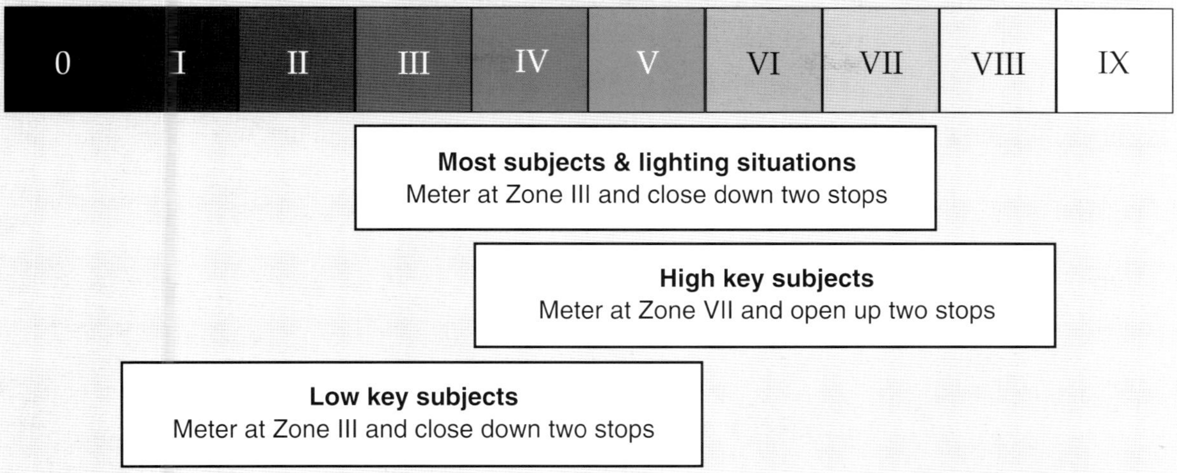

Figure 9 – The 'five-stop block' approach

our camera accordingly.

Note: When taking a meter reading always go right up to the chosen Zone to take the reading (when possible), but do not go so close as to cause a false reading from your own shadow.

Correct exposure is the most important discipline of all.

You need to learn, understand and master how to expose correctly.

If you don't, you will never acquire the level of control which is necessary to produce consistently high quality work.

Exposure control is critical because it directly affects the look of the finished print. Exposure deficiencies often show up in the shadow areas – whilst featureless black areas can add dramatic impact, they more often undermine the credibility of the print. Underexposed shadows (featureless black) or over-exposed highlights (featureless white) lack form and texture – elements which are usually essential in the 'make-believe' that a two-dimensional image represents a three-dimensional reality.

The only time you can achieve correct exposure is at the taking stage – if you fail then, you have lost it forever: the best you can achieve is a 'salvage operation' at the printing stage.

Exposure summary

When using the Zone System to determine correct exposure, proceed as follows:

1 Decide on the scene to be photographed and from what position.

2 Focus the camera on the most important part of the subject to be photographed.

3 Meter from the 'shadow' area in which you wish to show fully textured detail (usually Zone III).

4 Meter the textured 'highlight' area (Zone VII). Count how many 'Stops' (EVs) difference there are between the chosen textured shadow and highlight areas. If this is five stops, then use 'Normal' development; if not, we will need to make adjustments at the development stage.

5 Set the camera as indicated by the exposure meter for the selected textured shadow area; then close down the aperture by two stops (for example, if the meter reading was indicating 1/125 at f/8, then set the camera for 1/125 at f/16).

6 Press the shutter release.

That's about all there is to correct exposure. But remember it is the most constructive and important discipline. To progress with your work, you must become its master.

Summary of Lesson 2

In order to expose a film, it has to receive a given amount of light. This amount of light is referred to as its EXPOSURE INDEX (EI), which relates to the film's speed (measured as ISO numbers). The exposure meter needs to be set for the film speed.

An Exposure Value (EV) of 1=1 Stop, which =1 Zone, which =1 Tone.

One stop either doubles or halves the amount of light reaching the film or paper.

Exposure meters are calibrated from an 18% reflectance Kodak Grey Card and give the exposure needed to render anything we point it at as mid-grey.

We have to compensate for tonal variation in the scene/subject by opening up or closing down our camera's aperture from the reading indicated by our meter.

Where possible, it is preferable to meter from and expose for the textured shadow area of a scene/subject.

We should only meter from the fully textured Zones/Tones.

Correct exposure is correct exposure, no matter what type of films we use.

LESSON 3

Film Development

This lesson covers:

- Personal film speeds
- How to determine our own preferred/personal development time
- How to obtain our required negative density.

In the previous lesson, we introduced the adage 'Expose for the shadows and develop for the highlights'. Well, we've learnt how to expose for the shadows, so let's look at how to develop for the highlights.

For a given level of exposure, the time and temperature of the developer determines the density (thickness) of the negative. Exposure of the film when we take our photograph, determines the density (or lack of it) in the shadow areas. This in turn means that when the film is developed, the density of the negative is clear or translucent in the shadow areas. The effect of the developer (both time and temperature) is more apparent in the highlight areas of the film. The developer causes the silver halides to swell, which creates the opacity or thickness of the negative at the 'highlight' end. It is the degree of opacity which restricts the amount of light from the enlarger reaching the paper. Dense highlights in the negative mean that the paper receives little or no exposure, causing it to retain its whiteness.

Our skill as photographers is to control (a) the amount of light taken on board by the film during exposure, and (b) the amount of swelling that takes place in the halides during development.

You cannot produce a bright, clean sparkling print without first having a bright, clear sparkling negative.

So what we have to discover is the correct development time for the film to achieve the required density range in the negative.

All is not what it seems with regards to film speeds. Tests by many eminent photographers demonstrate conclusively that the optimum performance of virtually all panchromatic films (measured in terms of grain size and image sharpness) is achieved at a speed rating lower than that set by the manufacturers (the 'nominal' film speed).

As a rule of thumb, rating the film at half its nominal ISO speed will (provided compensation is made at the development stage) produce the optimum results. For example, an ISO 200 film would be rated at ISO 100 – this loses one stop in terms of film speed, but with correct development will result in the minimum possible evidence of grain in the final print. This is one of those facts that you can choose to accept or ignore – if you do decide to accept it, then set your chosen film speed before conducting your personal development time test as described in this lesson.

PERSONAL DEVELOPMENT TIMES

We are (thank goodness) all different – we use different equipment and different processing techniques, and we will have different preferences for negative density when printing. It is necessary, therefore, to find out your personal optimum development time which, even with the same film and chemicals, may differ from other photographers.

There are numerous ways in which you can determine your own personal development time (PDT). The important thing is to conduct this test under conditions where there is a five stop difference between the fully textured shadow area and the fully textured highlight area. This is the method I use to work out my own personal development time.

1) I took a white plant pot which had pebble dash sides and contained some plants. On a bright sunny day I placed the plant pot outside in the sunlight. I also placed (though this isn't necessary) a Kodak Grey Card and Step Wedge within the scene.

2) I took a meter reading from the soil area in shadow (fully textured shadow area). I then took a meter reading from the white pebble dash side which had the sunlight falling on it (fully textured highlight) – the range was five stops, which is just what I needed. Because I wanted to reproduce this tonality in my final print, it helped enormously that it existed in the first place. If you are establishing your own PDT, then ensure that this five stop range exists when carrying out the initial development tests.

3) I then loaded into my camera the film for which I wanted to establish my own PDT, and set my meter reading to my chosen film speed.

4) I placed my camera on a tripod, focused on the plant pot and took a meter reading for the fully textured shadow area.

5) From the meter reading, I closed down my lens by two stops (as explained in lesson 2), thus ensuring that I had exposed the film for the shadow area.

6) I shot off the whole roll of film on that one setting.

7) In the darkroom (with the lights out) I took the film out of my camera and using old ice cream containers as dishes for develop, stop and fixer, I proceeded to cut the film into six pieces. I then placed all the strips of film into the developer at once and set my clock going.

8) The manufacturer's recommended development time for this particular film in

this developer was 8 minutes. I based my times around this and developed my first strip for 7 minutes. I then took this strip out of the developer and placed it into the stop bath. At 8 minutes I took out my second strip and put one nick into the edge of the negative with a pair of scissors and then dropped this strip into the stop bath. I did the same at one minute intervals, placing one additional nick in the edge of each strip (ie the last strip had five nicks).

When all the strips had been developed and stopped, I placed them in the fix for the recommended time. When fixing was complete, I washed and dried the strips in the normal manner.

After drying, look at the highlight area of the individual strips until you find the highlight in which you can just see detail. The strip which contains this (Zone VII) detail is the strip which indicates your personal development time (PDT) for your chosen film when developed in your chosen developer. If you have included a Kodak Grey Card and Step Wedge in the scene then look in the shadow areas. If you can see tonal separation between the wedges, then you have exposed correctly. If you can see tonal separation of the highlight wedges then you have developed correctly. This is now your benchmark or datum point and should now be considered your NORMAL development time (NDT) or personal development time (PDT) for this film/developer combination and will remain so for as long as you want it to be. (You may decide to change this at a later date if you really start to fine tune your processing). REMEMBER We are aiming for consistency: therefore always use the same processing technique when developing films in future, ie mix the developer and water in the same proportions, use the same temperature and agitation techniques. Water varies in different areas, so do not develop your films away from your own locality and expect the same results.

This strip of negatives should now print easily on grade 2-2.5 paper, reproducing the full range of tones that were apparent at the taking stage.

You may wish to use another method to determine your own PDTs, but I do urge you to do this at the outset; it can save an awful lot of time later on.

Just for information (and as a comparison for your own tests), I have found the following film/developer combinations work for me:

Ilford FP4 Plus rated at ISO 50 and developed for 9.5 minutes.

Kodak T-Max 100, rated at ISO 100 and developed for 11.5 minutes.

Kodak T-Max 400, rated at ISO 400 and developed for 10 minutes.

In all instances I develop in Ilford ID11 1+1 (1 measure of water + 1 measure of developer) at 20°C. I fix the FP4 Plus for 4 minutes; however, I find that with T-Max film I have to fix for almost as long as I develop, otherwise the negatives fail to 'clear' properly leaving a slight fog.

I develop all my films in ID11. Occasionally I will use other films such as Agfa or Fuji, but I consider T-Max 100 and T-Max 400 to be my stock films. I have found that T-Max 400 meets most of my criteria and use this for the vast majority of my photographs. The grain is so minimal that it doesn't bother me. I even use it for my landscape work. The advantage of using ISO 400 film is that I can go out walking with just my Fuji 6x7 camera (this has a fixed standard lens) and a monopod. I can walk where I want to when I want to without the need for a pack mule to carry my equipment. The combination is very fast to use. I can react very quickly to rapid light changes and rarely miss a shot. It works for me, though it does have some limitations. However, the advantages far outweigh the disadvantages and my method of working seems to be causing many of my fellow photographers to re-think their own approach after seeing how simply I work and viewing the end results.

CONTRAST

Our personal development times are fine for normal lighting conditions, where there is a five stop range between fully textured shadows and highlights. In dull lighting, however, the range between fully textured shadows and highlights can be as little as three stops, whereas in bright sunlight with reflective surfaces and deep shadows, the range will exceed five stops.

If we go back to our tonal step wedge, we can see that we metered for the fully textured shadow area (Zone III). We then developed our film for the length of time necessary to obtain the amount of contrast required to build up the negative density to the stage where this density only just allows enough light to pass from the enlarger onto the printing paper. This area then prints as a fully textured highlight area (Zone VII). Theoretically, were we to print through this negative we should reproduce exactly the tones we require on normal grade paper (grade 2 or 2.5). We will cover paper grades in more detail in 'lesson' 4.

If you take exposure meter readings from shadow areas and highlight areas on a dull day, it is probable that you would find the meter reading would only display a 2 or 3 stop Zone/Tone difference between our determined shadow area and our visualised highlight area, rather than the desired 5 stop difference. If we develop the film normally, we will have a low contrast, 'flat' negative, because the development time would not be long enough to build up density in the highlight area to Zone VII (it would actually fall one Zone short on Zone VI). This is because the halides were not able to absorb sufficient developer to swell up enough to block out the required amount of light from the enlarger.

Because density is controlled by the development time, the solution is obvious: lengthen the development time to push our Zone VI up to Zone VII, allowing us to reproduce the desired range of tone in our final print. This is done

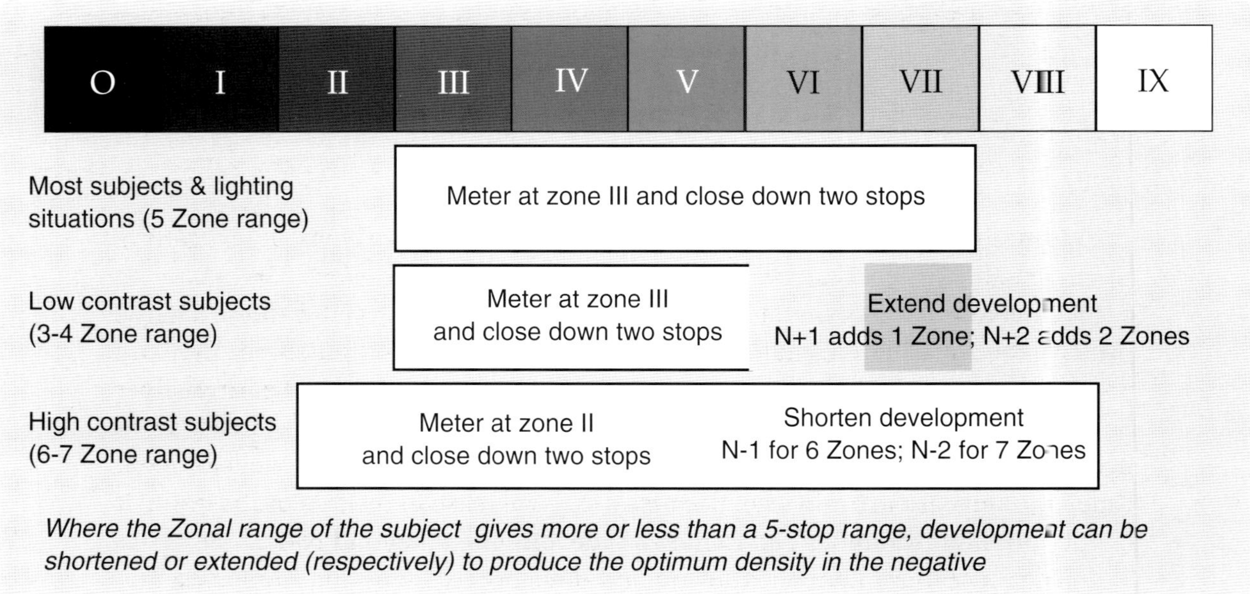

Figure 10 – Development compensation

without affecting the shadow areas of the negative, because the two aspects of exposure and development work virtually independently of each other. Each has little or no effect on the other. This fact allows us the wonderful facility to control the density values of our negative. Control of these values ultimately controls the destiny of our final print. Think about it, if the silver halides on the film did not collect any light from the subject's shadow areas when the film was exposed, then how can the film's developer expand these halides?

If we are aware at the taking stage that the required tonal contrast or brightness will not be available, then we can make the relevant decisions before taking the photograph. For example, do we increase or decrease development times, if so by how long,? Does this mean we now have to become embroiled in mind-blowing technicalities in order to make such decisions? The answer is most definitely 'no'.

There is a very simple formula from which to work. If the contrast values fall 1 stop short of the desired five stop range, increase development by 1 Stop. The new development time would now be referred to as N+1 (NDT +1 Stop). In other words, we are making good the 1 stop that we were short of when taking the photograph, thus bringing our tonal range back up to the golden 5 Stops. If the contrast range was only 3 stops between our visualised Zone III and our visualised Zone VII, then we would have to increase development time to N+2 (NDT + 2 stops).

Conversely, if the difference between our Zone III and Zone VII exceeds 5 stops on very bright days, we would need to reduce our development times in order to bring down our contrast range. If we failed to take this action, the negative highlight areas will be too dense ('blocked up') so that no detail would appear in the highlight areas of the print (ie 'paper base white'). The result of this is that the highlight areas of the print are blocked up and appear totally white showing no detail. As described above, undesired loss of detail in either the shadows or highlights tends to destroy the illusion or 'make-believe' of the print.

As a rule of thumb, the adjustment to development time for N+ or N- development is 20-30% per stop, depending on the type of film used:

5 stop measured contrast = Normal Development Time (N), eg 10 mins
Low contrast:
4 stop measured contrast = N+1 development (ie N+30%), eg 13 mins
3 stop measured contrast = N+2 development (ie N+1 + 30%), eg 16.9 mins
High contrast:
6 stop measured contrast = N-1 development (ie N-30%), eg 7 minutes
7 stop measured contrast = N-2 development (ie N-1 - 30%), eg 4.9 mins

N+1 development has no effect on the shadow areas: we have to start getting up to the mid tones before there is any effective impression. This starts to accelerate more rapidly when operating on the higher tonal values. This is because the silver halides in the shadow area did not gather light. Since they did not gather light, the chemical reaction of the developer on light bearing silver halides does not take place. This in turn means that the silver halides do not swell up to create density in the negative. The by-product of extended development time is an increase in grain size. Because of this increase in the size of the grain, it is not normally recommended to increase development beyond N+2.

The fortuitous effect of exposure and development working independently

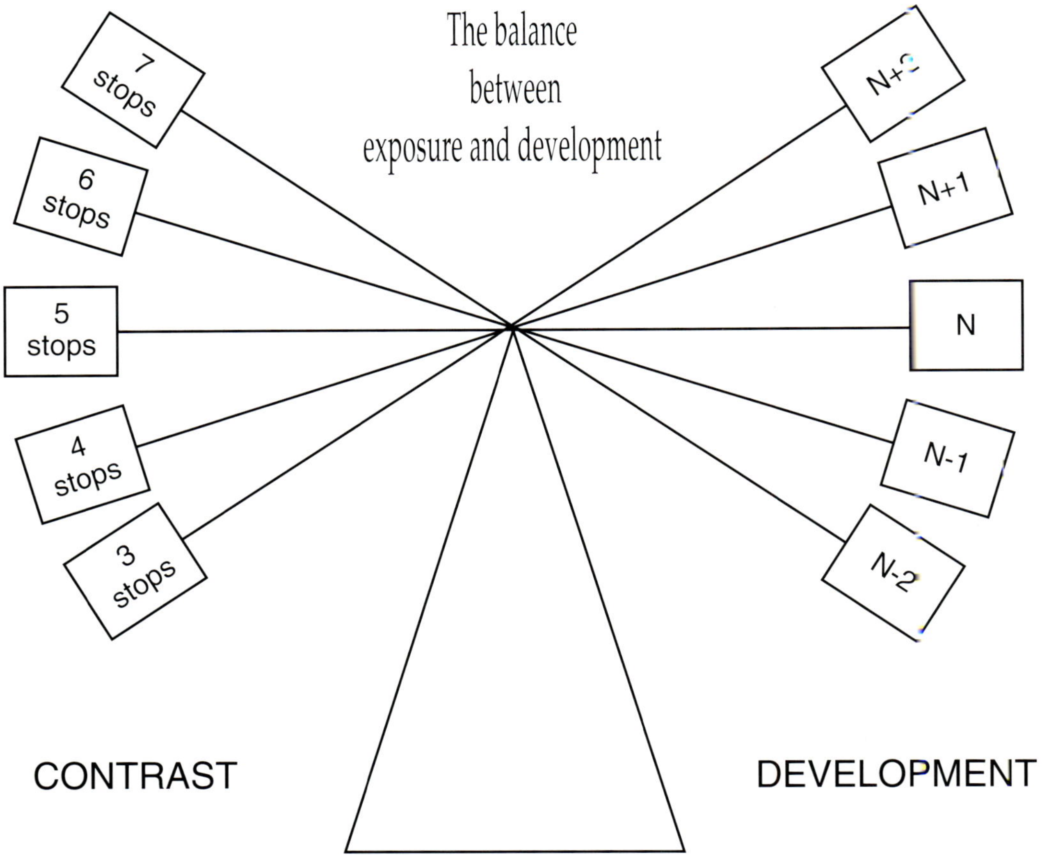

Think of the normal subject contrast (ie five fully textured stops) and normal development time as a balanced set of scales. A lower contrast subject tips the left side downwards, requiring a compensating increase in development (N+1 or N+2) to restore the balance. Conversely, a more contrasty subject will require less development to restore the balance. So, on dull days increase development to add contrast and under bright conditions reduce development to prevent burnt-out highlights.

Figure 11 – Balancing exposure and development

offers us tremendous flexibility and allows us to control precisely the degree of translucency and opacity in the negative to achieve the desired printed tones.

People almost always disbelieve that you can reduce film development time down to 4 minutes without causing problems in the shadow areas. They are convinced that the shadow areas will suffer and also be reduced as well as the highlights. This is not the case; only highlight areas are affected. Remember that exposure takes care of the shadows and therefore the transparency of the negative. We don't in fact want much density in the shadow areas at all if we are to achieve rich black and dark shadow areas. The development time will determine the opacity/density of the negative's highlights. Think the process through and I think you will agree, it is logical.

Many photographers give their films a 'little bit extra' in the developer to be 'on the safe side'. Under normal contrast conditions, this will result in the highlight areas becoming too opaque and printing either as paper base white or without the visualised Zone VII texture. You can get round this by burning-in (giving extra exposure to) these areas during the printing process – but excessive burning-in usually results in the highlight area having a muddy grey appearance rather than a fully textured bright white highlight.

You cannot have a bright sparkling print if you don't have a bright sparkling negative to start with. Now we know how to obtain such a negative. Just think: we can now determine how our final print will appear before we fire the camera shutter. Eureka!

We've basically covered film development. You can see from the various illustrations and examples used in this lesson the effects of increasing/expanding development. In nearly every case we need to aim for the 5 'Golden' Stops between the Zone III shadow area and the Zone VII highlight area (provided this is how you pre-visualised the scene/subject, and that this is how you wish it to be recorded in your final print).

So far we have covered the 'ideal' scenario where the film development is geared precisely to the contrast range of the subject: in practice, we could only achieve this ideal with sheet film, where we use a separate sheet of film for each photograph taken, developing it individually according to the conditions prevailing at the time of exposure.

For users of roll films, such as 35mm and 120, then we do regrettably have to compromise. Obviously, if an entire film is exposed under similar lighting and contrast conditions, it should be possible to match the development to the tonal range required. For this reason, some monochrome photographers will use different camera bodies for films to be developed at N, N+1 or N-1. Similarly, many medium format cameras have interchangeable backs, so it is possible to keep backs marked for the different development times. Any slight deviations between negatives on such films can be readily addressed in the darkroom by our choice of paper grade when printing (more about paper grades later).

Summary of Lesson 3

It is necessary to discover your own personal development time for a given film and developer combination. As a starting point, try halving the manufacturer's ISO rating and reducing the recommended development time by 30%.

Whilst exposure governs shadow detail, film development controls the correct negative density for the Zone VII highlight area.

Where the tonal range of a subject is less or greater than five stops, we need to compensate by adjusting film development times.

The overriding point comes back to exposure for the shadows and development for the highlights: meter the textured shadow area of your subject and close down by two stops; extend development for low contrast subjects and shorten development for high contrast subjects. That, in essence, is the key to getting bright negatives which will readily produce sparkling prints. ***If you do nothing more than put into practice the content of this paragraph, you will begin to see a marked improvement in the technical quality of your prints.***

LESSON 4

Basics of Printing

I am assuming that readers are reasonably familiar with basic darkroom procedures and printing techniques. However, to ensure that terminology is understood, this lesson covers some of the key aspects:

- Various types of photographic paper
- How to determine the paper's maximum black
- Some terminology and techniques used in the darkroom
- Types of paper developers.

TYPES OF PAPER

We basically only need to concern ourselves with two types of paper for printing: resin coated (RC) and fibre-based (FB).

Resin Coated is a plastic based paper whose prime advantage is that of speed. It is quick to process and dry. It dries flat and is quite hard to damage, though glossy surfaces can scratch easily. It does not lend itself readily to 'invisible' spotting (see later).

On the other hand, fibre-based paper is more delicate and creases easily if not handled properly. It requires a lot of washing and takes a long time to dry. It does not dry flat naturally. On the plus side, it spots readily and has a richness and depth of tone that resin coated paper cannot, in my opinion, match. Fibre-based papers look superb and have a sensuous feel which offers an extra dimension to the final image. Properly processed and stored, a fibre-based print is archivally permanent.

Generally speaking, resin coated papers are ideal for proof and working prints, whereas most serious photographers prefer fibre-based prints for exhibition and presentation purposes.

Each of the above types of paper are available either in fixed contrast grades or in variable contrast (VC) or multigrade (MG) versions. (VC and MG are synonymous.) Fixed grades relate to the contrast of the paper – if you want to change the contrast of the print, you will need to have boxes of each grade of paper available.

With multigrade, the one paper is capable of covering all the necessary grades simply by changing the filtration of the enlarger light. It also has the advantage that several grades can in fact be used on a single print (split grading). In the most popular paper ranges, multigrade paper has now taken over from fixed grades because of its versatility and the fact that only one box of paper needs to be stocked. However, some of the most exciting 'art' papers are only available in fixed grades.

Paper grades

These are generally numbered from Grade 0 through to Grade 5 in half grade increments. Grade 0 is very soft and accommodates a very dense negative, offering a very full range of tones. Grade 5 is a very hard grade of paper, printing almost as just black and white. It is normally used when a very thin negative lacking tonal contrast has to be printed. Not all graded papers are offered in a full range of grades – quite often only in grades 2 ('normal' contrast) and 3 ('hard').

Choice of paper

We are fortunate to have a wide range of papers to choose from. Apart from the multigrade/fixed grade and resin coated/fibre distinctions, the main differences between papers are in the emulsion coating, the colour of the paper base and the type of surface.

Like film, papers are coated with a light-sensitive emulsion. The chemical composition of this coating varies and this, in combination with the reaction to the paper developer, affects the 'colour' of the tones in the print. This gives the printer choice between 'warm', 'neutral' and 'cold' tones of black. The emulsion also affects the 'speed' (light-sensitivity) of the paper and its subsequent reaction to use of toners.

Most papers have a white base, but the degree to which these vary can be surprising. Like paper emulsions, they can vary in warmth and this will be reflected in the 'feel' of the print. Some papers are distinctly off-white: a cream coloured base being quite popular in the art paper ranges, for example.

The most common surfaces are glossy, semi-matt or pearl, and matt, although there are variants such as fine lustre and the textured art finishes. Note that whereas resin-coated glossy papers are quite shiny when dry, glossy fibre papers dry to a relatively dull sheen unless 'glazed' (a process whereby the surface is heat-dried against a shiny aluminium plate to form a rich gloss).

All of these variables – emulsion, paper base and surface – will affect the impact of the finished print. For the fine printer, part of the skill is in choosing the paper which best matches the mood he or she is trying to create within the image. It is tempting therefore to accumulate shelves full of part used boxes of paper (which do deteriorate over time even though they do not usually carry a 'use by' date). However, particularly when starting out on the fine print route, it is helpful to eliminate as many variables as possible. I suggest that when you start, you pick one good quality paper – such as Ilford Multigrade IV or the excellent Kentmere multigrade papers (my personal preference) – and get to know it well. When you have mastered fine printing using that paper, you have set a standard by which to compare your experiments with other papers.

Getting to know your paper is almost as important as understanding your film and developer combination fully. It helps you to pre-visualise how the colourful three-dimensional subject in front of your camera will translate into a monochromatic two-dimensional sheet of paper. As you gain experience, of course, you will start to anticipate the type of paper and finishing processes which will best suit a particular subject even before you make the exposure.

Characteristic curves

In Lesson 2 we saw a typical characteristic curve for film after development. A virtually identical graph can be produced showing the characteristic curve for the printing paper:

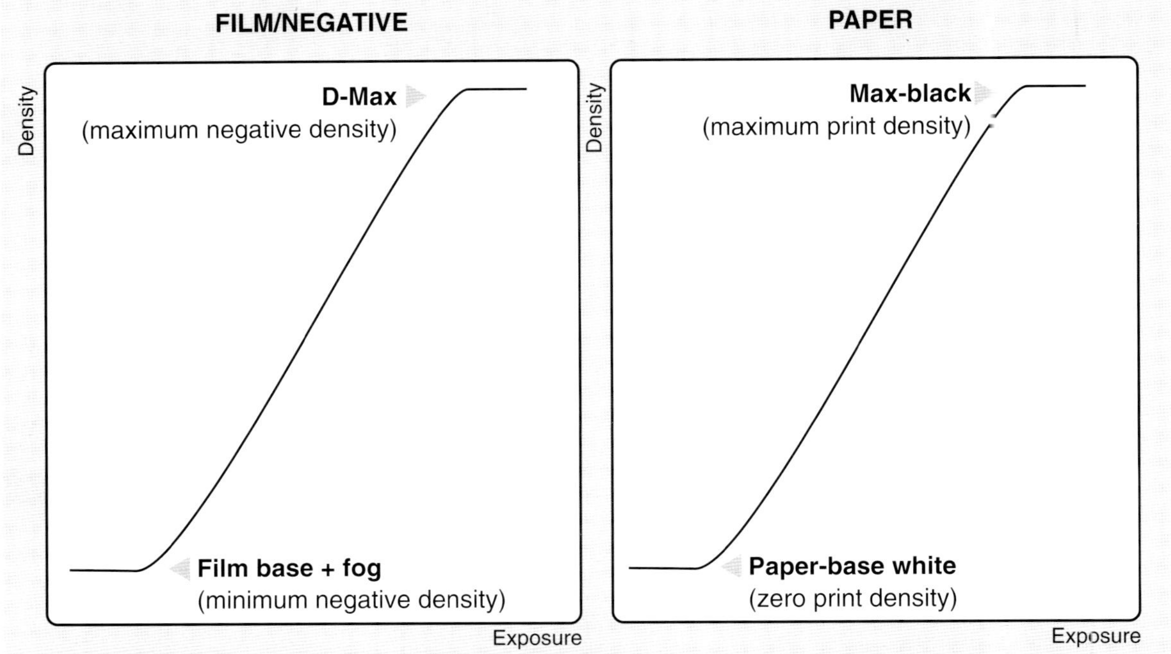

Figure 12 – Characteristic curves for film and paper

We can see from the characteristic curves that a maximum black is produced on the paper by printing through the thinnest part of the negative, film base + fog. Of course, if we over-expose other tones sufficiently, they could also be printed as maximum black. Maximum whiteness (the white of the paper base) in the print is achieved through having maximum density on the negative, which prevents sufficient light from the enlarger passing through the negative to register a tone on the paper. Again, under-exposing other tones can also render them as paper base white on the print.

When printing, it is a good idea to remember or be aware of how a water colour artist would use paper and paints. In order to create highlight areas on his/her painting, the artist simply leaves the relevant area of the paper untouched (or only slightly touched). This effectively leaves the desired area its natural basic colour (paper base white). In order to add density to his/her work the artist builds up the colours from the basic white colour of the paper. This is done by mixing various other colours and then applying these to other parts of the painting, this therefore adds density to the painting. As photographers, we can do the same with our printing. We need to learn how to control the amount of light that reaches the printing paper in the highlight areas of the photograph. By doing this, we are able to control the amount of detail that we wish to display in these highlight areas. We need to control this in order that we may leave the chosen areas of the print either paper base white or as close to paper base white as we choose. In other words, the first thing that we have to learn as printers is how to control the exposure of the paper for the highlight areas of the print.

We build up the blacks or shadow areas to suit ourselves and how we wish the final image to appear. We do this by selecting the grade of paper to suit our shadow areas. A low paper grade gives 'soft' shadow areas; conversely, a harder grade of paper gives very dark and 'hard' shadows. It is good practice to determine the maximum black that the paper of your choice is capable of producing. To do this we need to know the minimum exposure time to produce maximum black.

Determining the max black threshold point
To determine this minimum exposure time to achieve maximum black for any given make of paper at a specific level of enlargement:

1) Place a piece of unexposed developed negative (ie film base + fog density) into the enlarger negative carrier;

2) Set the enlarger column to the desired height;

3) Place a sheet of the printing paper in the easel;

4) Close down the enlarger lens by 2 stops from the widest aperture;

5) Cover all of the paper except for half an inch (12mm) with a piece of card and expose for one second;

6) Carry on moving the card down the sheet of paper in half inch (12mm) increments and keep exposing the paper for one (1) second at a time;

7) Do this right to the bottom of the paper leaving the last half inch (12mm) unexposed;

8) Develop and process the paper in the normal way ensuring that full development takes place, usually 2 minutes for resin coated paper or 3 minutes for fibre based paper (check the paper developer instructions);

9) Fully dry the paper and then count up from the unexposed strip how many seconds exposure have taken place before you fail to see any further change.

Say this proves to be 8 seconds; this then is your minimum exposure time for maximum black on the chosen type and grade of paper at the chosen aperture and column height of the enlarger head. Knowing this threshold point is useful for controlling the tones in a print, particularly if you have shadow areas in which you wish to retain a hint of detail without going to max-black.

BASIC PRINTING TECHNIQUES

Printing really is quite simple provided the negative has good tonality. Nonetheless there are various techniques which can be used to enhance the quality of a print. These form part of the printer's language:

Dodging (or holding back)
This is where we prevent (hold back) light from the enlarger reaching a certain part of a print during exposure. Dodging therefore makes an area of the print lighter than it would otherwise be. Normally, this is done by using a small piece

of black card on the end of a thin wire ('wand'). This card is then waved briefly above the area in question: moving the card produces a gentle gradation around the edges of the dodged area. If you make the sort of test sheet described above for determining max-black, you can use this to see the effect on any tone of successive seconds of dodging.

Burning-in

This is done to give additional exposure to or darken certain parts of the print. Usually this is done by cutting a hole in a piece of card which is big enough to block extra light getting to other areas of the print; sometimes using the edge of a sheet card is more appropriate (eg when burning-in sky detail).

Probably the most common use of burning-in is to reproduce detail which is on the negative but which the paper cannot reproduce without some help – highlight details and skies, for example. But burning-in can be used to add mystique to an image, or to balance tonal areas in the composition, or to direct the viewer's eye to a certain part of the image.

The aim of good exposure and development practice is to minimise the need for dodging and burning – these should normally be for fine-tuning purposes rather than to salvage a print from a poor negative. The more dodging and burning you have to do, the more likely it will leave tell-tale signs in the print (such as muddy highlights or strained shadows).

I remember one character at a camera club talk I was giving saying to me "If that Ansel Adams was so good, how come he had to do all that dodging and burning-in". Well, the answer is as explained above. The negative's capacity for detail is far greater than that of the paper. Therefore as printers we have to master how best to impart this detail from the negative onto the paper.

Pre-flashing

This is a technique whereby we expose the paper very briefly to a small controlled amount of light prior to printing. It is used more frequently on graded papers in order to give more control of the highlight areas when printing; say, for example, that a print looks too soft on a grade 3 paper and too hard on a grade 4 paper, then pre-flashing would soften the grade 4 paper down to roughly grade 3.5.

The exact time that a paper needs to be 'flashed' is determined by conducting a series of one second exposures on one piece of paper: process and dry in the normal fashion and then look for the last strip that is paper base white (pre fogged) just prior to the one that has turned grey (fogged). Count how many seconds exposure have taken place (this generally is around 2-4 seconds) up to the last white band and this then is your determined flashing time. This varies not only from paper to paper but also from grade to grade. Some printers say that with multigrade papers flashing is obsolete, others will disagree. I personally have not flashed a piece of paper for years. (See 'threshold printing' below).

Types of paper developers

These are too numerous to detail and the final choice always is down to the individual. The choice of developer can affect both the colour of the print and the contrast. It may seem strange to talk about the colour of a monochrome print, but (depending also on the paper), this can vary between a cold blue-black and a warm brown-black – which will be appropriate depends both on the subject content and personal preference.

I personally only consider hard developers and soft developers. Generally, I find that if I am using a hard grade of paper, the soft developer works better, whilst soft grades seem to respond better to a harder developer. Each works differently on the highlights of the print. I must say that after working for a number of years with soft and hard developers I have reverted back to using just one developer (primarily due to lack of space in my darkroom for all the 12 x 16 trays required when using fibre based paper). The one I choose is Ilford's good old PQ Universal, a quite superb developer which can be diluted according to your personal requirements, though I mainly use the dilution recommended by the manufacturer, ie 1+9. Personally I cannot detect significant tonal changes in my prints since reverting back to PQ and wonder if I was searching for something that was not there in the first place. Maybe, like a lot of other things, one's personal evolution brings you back to where you started, but hopefully with a significantly improved knowledge and understanding.

Spotting

When printing, any specks of dust that were evident on the negative or any of the horizontal surfaces which lie in the enlarger's light path will result in small light spots appearing on the final print. These spots need to be removed and we do so by applying spotting dyes.

Spotting is a technique which most definitely needs to be practised and worked on. I put a tiny amount of spotting dye in an old saucer and allow this to dry thoroughly on the saucer before use. When I need to spot, I take my spotting brush, lightly rub this on the edge of a slightly moist sponge and then just touch the almost dry brush onto my spotting dye. Before proceeding to touch the offending spot, just touch the white border of the print (or use a discarded print or test strip made with the same paper) to ensure that the colour match is correct and also to ensure that the brush is not too heavily loaded.

Spotting requires patience. Use repeated dabs of the pointed brush on the spot and gradually build-up the required density. Above all, keep your brush as dry as practicable – have it too wet and the dye will form a ring around the edge of the spotted area, accentuating the spot rather than removing it.

I wrote earlier that printing is quite simple, provided that we have the required negative values. It is amazing how many people ask me to show them how to print or even state that their weakness lies in their printing. My experience has shown me that the problem is usually with exposure and development of the film rather than with printing technique. The tonal values and placements are wrong through a combination of both incorrect exposure and/or incorrect development. I know some people do not mind spending all evening trying to obtain a good print. But I cannot personally see the advantage in spending a whole evening trying to achieve what can be done in an hour or so provided the negative is good and we know how to print.

How do we print? Well this is very subjective and every printer will advise you differently. I can only explain, therefore, how I print and hope that the logic of my explanation will be understood. In essence, I use the Gene Nocon F-Stop method of printing, which I find suits my style but also, importantly, always gives me a good basic set of procedures from which to work. In Lesson 5 I will explain this method of working.

Summary of Lesson 4

In this lesson we have covered:

• Types of papers, eg resin coated and fibre based, fixed grade and variable contrast (or 'multigrade')

• How to determine the maximum black of the paper and the threshold for paper base white

• Dodging and burning-in to control density in local areas of a print

• Flashing

• Spotting

• Different types of paper developer.

We have also seen that when printing we expose for the highlights and we then bring in the shadow detail by choice of paper grade. This will be covered in more detail in the next lesson.

LESSON 5

Printing technique

In this lesson we will cover:

- The Gene Nocon F-stop method of printing
- How to determine basic print exposure times
- How to determine choice of paper grades.

GENE NOCON F-STOP METHOD OF PRINTING

American master printer Gene Nocon developed the F-stop method of printing which, in essence, is yet another way of working within a disciplined manner. The benefit being that if something goes wrong, it is easy to retrace your steps to find out where it went wrong and thus take corrective measures.

By working to the F-stop method of printing, we basically carry over into the darkroom the Zone System. By starting at a basic point, we can expose very easily to within 1/4 stop. Were we to expose our film within a 1/4 stop then we would be delighted, so why not carry this over to our darkroom practice and expose our paper to within 1/4 stop (or less!)?

Let's assume that you are printing a landscape scene which contains foreground detail and white fluffy clouds. The F-stop method is as follows:

1) Set up your negative in the enlarger's negative carrier in the normal way, focus and close down the lens.

2) Select the enlarger filtration for paper grade 2.5, as this is a good mid-range paper grade (with experience, observation of the negative density will indicate which paper grade to choose for your initial test strips).

3) Take a piece of paper from its box and tear this in half, putting one half back in the box safe from light.

4) Place the retained piece in the masking frame and cover up half this piece with card and expose the remaining half for 5 seconds.

5) Cover half of this exposed area and expose for a further 5 seconds. (The sequence of exposures is much clearer from the diagram in Figure 13 than from my attempt at a written explanation!)

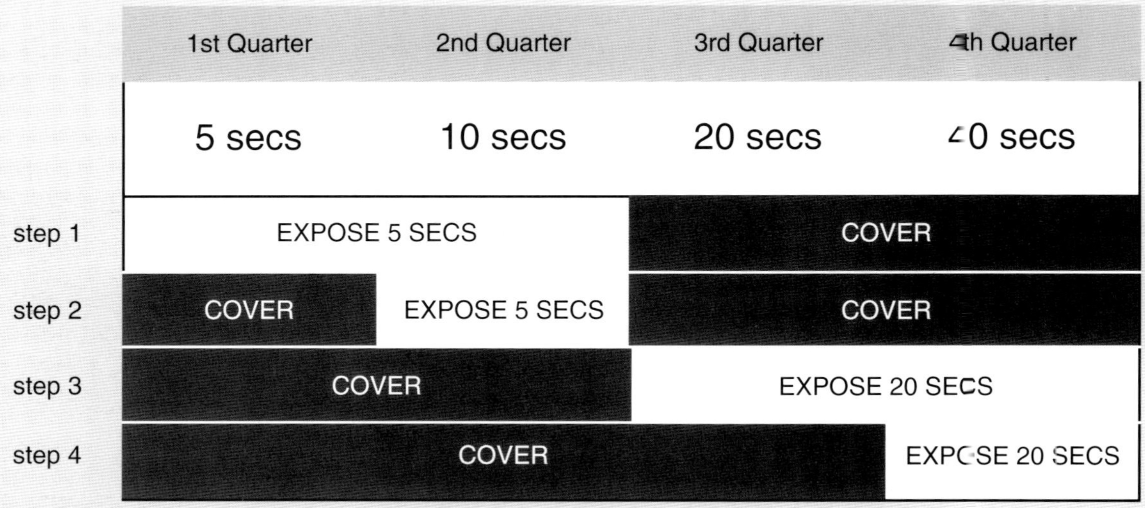

Figure 13 – Exposing the test strip, doubling the exposure (ie increasing by one stop) for each successive quarter

6) With another piece of card cover up the half of the paper which has already been exposed. Then take away the first card (ie leaving the right-hand half of the paper uncovered as shown in figure 13). Re-set your timer to 20 seconds and expose the paper for 20 seconds.

7) Finally move the card to the left leaving the last quarter uncovered and expose this for a further 20 seconds.

We now have each successive quarter of the piece of paper exposed for 5, 10, 20 and 40 seconds (ie each exposure is one stop more than the previous one). Develop, stop and fix the paper normally, then wash and dry. At this stage, only examine the 'highlight' area of the test strips. We are only looking for the correct highlight detail. Forget the shadows completely for the time being.

Some printers will subdivide the above into five sections, giving the final segment 80 seconds exposure in order that they may explore further the potential of the print. I have not found this necessary for my style of printing, so this is something for individuals to determine for themselves.

Some photographers say that this method of working is time-consuming and unnecessary. Needless to say, I don't agree: this method is especially helpful for the landscape photographer, where sky detail comes into the photograph. The time spent here will enable the printer to see exactly how much extra time (measured in f-stops) to give to the sky in order to fully realise its potential. Also, as I said earlier, following a set of procedures is good photographic technique. By using and referring to 'stops' when printing we can 'home in' very quickly to somewhere near where we need to be.

We may find that the exposure we require is somewhere between 10 and 20 seconds: at 10 seconds the print looks too weak (light) and at 20 seconds it looks too strong (dark). Figure 15 shows the range of intermediate quarter-stop exposures we could choose. For example, if we needed one quarter stop more than 10 seconds, we would increase the base exposure to 11.9 seconds. This becomes the starting point for our second test strip (using the other half of the original piece of paper).

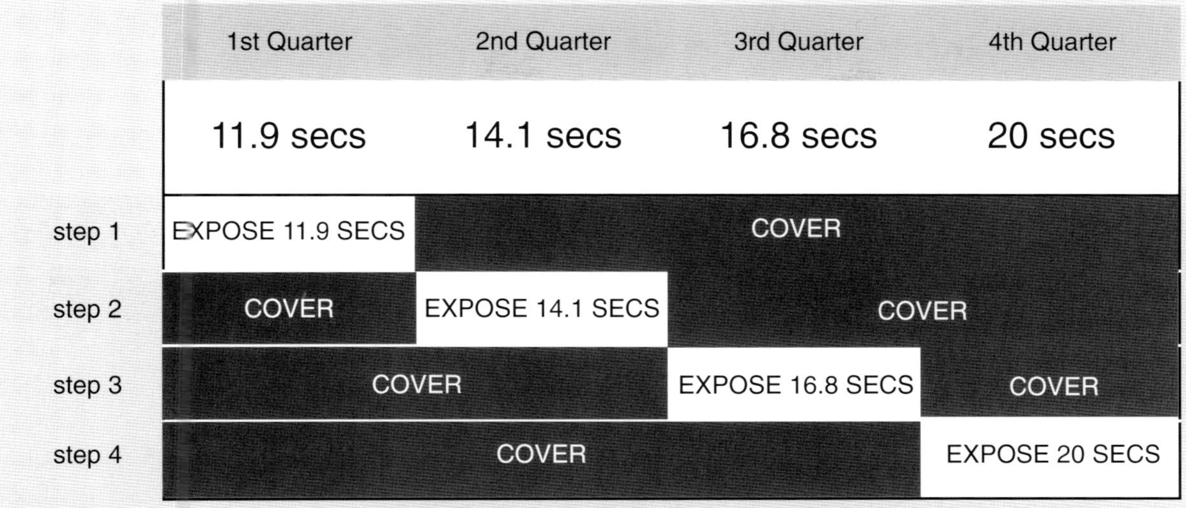

Figure 14 – Exposing the second test strip, increasing the exposure in quarter stops from the new base exposure of 11.9 seconds

To make the second test strip, place the second half of the original piece of paper in the easel and expose each segment in quarter stop increments, as shown in figure 14. I prefer to expose each segment in turn for the full exposure. I find this is much more accurate and easier to control than the alternative 'progressive exposure' method (where the whole sheet would be exposed for 11.9 seconds; one quarter is then covered and the rest exposed for another 2.2 seconds; then another quarter is covered and the remaining half exposed for 2.7 seconds and finally one quarter is left uncovered for another 3.2 seconds). Although the latter method, if applied successfully, will give the same exposure to each segment as in figure 14, it allows (in my opinion) too much room both for arithmetical error and for timer inaccuracies at shorter exposures.

Having processed and viewed the 1/4 stop 'fine tuned' exposures, we are in a position to assess and decide which exposure to select (even at this stage, if we find one segment too light and the next too dark, we can yet again sub-divide).

PRINT EXPOSURE TIME IS DETERMINED FROM THE HIGHLIGHT AREA OF THE SUBJECT

We can also view our first test strip which was exposed at full stops and study to see if there are any areas which obviously require extra exposure. For example, using our landscape example, we might find that our basic exposure needed to be somewhere around 10 seconds, but we can also see on the same strip that our sky area contained insufficient cloud detail at this exposure. From the test strip, we could find that the sky had the right tonal values at 40 seconds – so we know that the sky would need an extra two stops exposure above our base exposure time in order to realise its full potential and render correct balance to the print. This takes away any guesswork at the burning-in stage.

Having fine tuned our basic exposure time, we can now observe the shadow areas and other details of the print. We can now make our decision on choice of paper grade.

F-Stop 'Ready Reckoner'

Full stops	5	10	20	40	80
Quarter stops	5.9	11.9	23.8	47.6	95.2
Half stops	7.1	14.1	28.3	56.6	113.2
Three-quarter stops	8.4	16.8	33.6	67.3	134.6

To save mental arithmetic every time this method of printing is used, the following chart may be useful to add to or subtract from the base times:

Full stops	5	10	20	40	80
Quarter stops	0.9	1.9	3.8	7.6	15.2
Half stops	1.2	2.2	4.5	9.0	18.0
Three-quarter stops	1.3	2.7	5.3	10.7	21.4
(Full stop	*1.6*	*3.2*	*6.4*	*12.7*	*25.4)*

Figure 15 – F-stop 'ready reckoner'

CHOICE OF PAPER GRADE IS DETERMINED BY THE SHADOW AREA OF THE SUBJECT

We do this simply by looking at the detail in the shadow areas of the photograph. If the shadow detail is as we would like and expect, then we would leave our choice of paper grade exactly the same as the one chosen for the test print. However, if we find that the blacks in the shadow area are too dark and the detail is blocked out, then we would need to use a softer grade of paper. On the other hand, if we find that the shadow area is not deep enough and looks wishy-washy, then we would need to choose a harder grade of paper. The lower the paper grade, the softer the contrast – at the extremes, grade 0 is very soft and grade 5 is very hard.

Harder grades of paper give greater contrast and tonal separation than softer papers and are generally used when the negative is 'thin'. Soft grades of paper produce a beautiful soft gradation of tones and are generally used when the negative is dense. It is our negative density and contrast which determines which paper grade we have to use (unless we are deliberately choosing a grade of paper to give a particular artistic effect or mood).

Note that the filtration used with variable contrast papers can change the required exposure when changing grades (when compared with the test print).

Look at the information we have gained so far. We now know:

- Our basic exposure

- We can determine with reasonable accuracy where we need to give extra exposure by burning-in and by how much.

- If our choice of paper grade is correct.

All this information and we are still only on our first sheet of paper.

At this stage, I would suggest that should another choice of paper grade be made, it is sensible to make another test strip – remember, we are aiming at a fine print rather than a print 'that will do'. Paper speeds can vary between batches and, despite what variable contrast paper manufacturers tend to suggest, the required exposure is likely to vary marginally even if you make slight alterations to filtration to change grades. Alternatively, you could just process a small strip of paper of the preferred grade at the expected base exposure to confirm that no adjustment is necessary – discarding wasted sheets of paper is not just a waste of time and money, it is disheartening: when things start going wrong in the darkroom, they have a habit of continuing to do so!

If we find that our first test strip meets our expectations, then we can make our first full size print.

We simply print this for our determined basic exposure and burn-in as we feel fit from our test strips, and then process in the normal manner. When processing is complete and the print is dry, we have the first full size print that we can observe in its entirety. This first full size print is referred to as the print 'map' – it is the basis for deciding what further enhancement is possible by using our dodging and burning-in techniques. Some photographers will actually mark on the prints the areas to be dodged or burned-in and the timing for each area – if you don't want to mark the print, you can place it in a clear-faced negative bag and use a spirit-based marker pen on the outside of the bag.

Having made our decisions, we can proceed to produce our first 'master print' by exposing, dodging and burning-in as determined. Following processing, we should now have in front of us a beautiful finished fine art print – one to be proud of. And if we have made all the right decisions, we have only used three pieces of paper.

To summarise:

1) The first piece of paper was torn in half and one half was used to gauge the approximate exposure (eg 5, 10, 20, 40 seconds).

2) The second half of the first sheet of paper was used to fine-tune exposure time to within one quarter of a stop. From these first exposures we are usually able to evaluate paper grades and any areas that require additional exposure.

3) The second piece of paper was then used to produce a print map whereby we were able to determine where and by how much we needed to dodge and burn-in selected areas of the print.

4) The third (and hopefully the last) piece of paper is used for the final print, exposed, dodged and burned-in accordingly.

Sounds too easy? It really does work – try it!

Stop gap measurments
It can be seen from the chart on page 40 that a 1/4 stop more than 10 seconds is an extra 1.9 seconds, not 2.5 as would be assumed. This is because the increases are logarithmic rather than a straight proportional relationship.

Recalculating exposure for different print sizes
Working in f-stops is particularly helpful when making prints of different sizes from the same negative. If the sky needs three stops burning-in on a small print, it will also need three stops burning-in at bigger sizes (although these stops would be related to a longer basic exposure). If you simply made timed measurements for burning-in on the smaller print, it would be more difficult to recalculate the required burning-in at larger print sizes.

When moving from one size of enlargement to another, the required base exposure will obviously change. You can work out the new exposure by repeating the test strip exercise or you can get out a calculator and do some sums using the following formula:

$T2 = 2(L2/L1) \times T1$ WRONG $T_2 = (L_2/L_1)^2 \times T_1$

where: $L1$ = length of original image (not paper size)
$L2$ = length of new image (not paper size)
$T1$ = original exposure time
$T2$ = new exposure time

For example, if the original image was 9 inches long with an exposure time of 10 seconds, a print of 15 inches length would require roughly 28 seconds:

$$\begin{aligned} T2 &= 2(15/9) \times 10 \\ &= 2.778 \times 10 \\ &= 27.78 \text{ secs} \end{aligned}$$

T2 is rounded to the nearest quarter f-stop time (28.3 seconds) to give the new basic exposure time.

SOME HINTS ON PRINTING

Here are a few tips which I have found helpful:

1) Treat yourself to a decent set of print tongs. There is nothing more frustrating after having put a lot of effort into a print than having it slip out of a cheap pair of tongs and ending up as a crumpled mess.

2) After processing and washing your print, lay it on flat surface such as a piece of glass (make sure that all the edges of the glass are smoothed and that it is larger than the print). Wipe the print very gently with a soft squeegee blade (the type

that window cleaners use) to remove the surface water. Removing the excess water brings down the highlight tones and these appear much nearer the tonality of the dry print. This aids exposure assessment.

3) When viewing prints in the 'dry area', have a small desk lamp fitted with a 60 Watt daylight balanced bulb. It makes print assessment easier. Place the lamp at least 3ft (1 metre) from the print when viewing and, if possible, make it operable from a footswitch.

Summary of Lesson 5

This lesson has focused on:

1) The Gene Nocon F Stop printing method and its advantages.

2) Deciding on the basic exposure time by reference to the highlight areas.

3) Using the shadow details to determine what paper grade should be used.

4) We have also looked at how to interpret the large amount of detail that is available to use from our preliminary test strips.

Just as exposure and development of the film work independently of each other, so do print exposure and choice of paper grade. Isolate the two and think of them as independent controls. We are now getting to the stage where we can control all the elements of our photography, from the taking and development stage of the film through to the finished print. In the next lesson, we will look in particular at two further controls which are available to us.

LESSON 6

Refining printing control

This lesson looks at two ways in which we can build on the basic skills of the Nocon method, described in the previous chapter, to fine-tune our print control:

- Threshold printing
- Split-grade printing.

THRESHOLD PRINTING

The principle of monochrome printing is that the emulsion coated on the paper base reacts with light, so that when the paper is developed the more light that has reached a certain area, the darker will be the tone of that area in the print. However, if you look at the characteristic curve on page 32, you will see that there is a certain amount of exposure required before any tone (image density) appears at all, ie the paper can remain paper-base white even with some small amount of exposure to light. The longest amount of exposure before the paper starts to show any image density is described as the 'threshold point'.

The principle is much the same as pre-flashing the paper to reduce contrast with graded papers and to bring out highlight detail. However, pre-flashing is normally done without the negative in place. If you are using the same enlarger for the pre-flash and the main exposure, this is quite fiddly and time-consuming with plenty of opportunity for error.

Threshold printing is done with the negative in place and gives us greater control over the fine-tuning of the print. However, it does mean that we have to find where the threshold point is for any particular paper. To explain how to find the threshold point, we will assume that we have a landscape negative with a dense sky area (but one which does contain detail):

1) Set up the enlarger in the normal way with the negative in place. Focus and close down the lens. Select the enlarger filtration to grade 0.

2) Put half a piece of paper in the easel in the sky area and set the enlarger timer to expose for one second intervals.

3) Make a test strip, exposing each segment for one additional second. Process and dry in the normal manner.

4) When the test strip is dry, look for the strip that just shows highlight detail. The threshold point is one second less than this exposure.

The threshold point is your basic exposure time for the highlights: this will now give us greater control over the highlight detail in the print.

SPLIT-GRADE PRINTING

Exposing the paper at a soft grade up to the threshold point ensures that the paper is not fogged, so we will not get 'veiled' highlights. It brings the highlight areas up to a point where any additional exposure of light will register a tone containing detail from the negative.

The next stage is to determine our print times and paper grade for the rest of the print. This exposure will be made with a higher grade of contrast which will determine the overall range of tones in the print. To determine the second exposure and contrast setting, proceed as follows:

1) With the negative in place and contrast set to grade 0, expose half a piece of paper for the threshold printing time (determined as described above).

2) Reset the enlarger filtration to about one grade higher than your normal preferred contrast setting. Make a test strip as described in the F. Stop printing lesson. In other words, we are going to ascertain our full stop printing times, eg 5, 10, 20 and 40 seconds, as before. Process and dry in the normal manner.

3) Observe and determine which test strip gives the nearest results to the one required and then conduct the fine tuning test strip at 1/4 stop intervals as previously described. (Don't forget to first expose the paper on Grade 0 at the threshold printing time.) Process and dry the paper in the normal manner.

4) We should now have a strip which contains all the detail we require in the foreground and this determines our second (main) exposure time and contrast setting. If you are not happy with the shadow detail (either too flat or too stark), you will need to change the contrast for the second exposure (to a higher or lower grade respectively) and make a further test strip.

From the F Stop test strip, it is likely that the sky detail will look better in one of the exposures which is longer than the main second exposure. The test strip will indicate how many stops of additional exposure in that area will be required (by burning-in). Don't worry that giving this area more exposure will affect the delicate highlight detail, it won't. Only the darker areas will be effected.

This application of split-grade printing technique is effectively controlling print tones by painting with light. I said earlier that the water-colour painter would leave the highlight area of his or her paper untouched in order to create a highlight area in the painting. In essence we have done the same by printing to paper threshold on grade 0. The painter would build up contrast by applying extra layers of paint. Again, in essence, so have we. By moving up to a harder grade of paper and giving the paper a second exposure, we too have built up the tonal values and relative contrast in the print.

I have found on numerous occasions when printing delicate highlight detail that threshold printing times can be down to 1/10 or 2/10 of a second. Go beyond this time and your highlights will degrade. Remain on the right side of the threshold and your prints will contain bright sparkling highlight detail. It's a bit like standing on the edge of a cliff: stay at the edge on terra firma and you are safe; go that little bit further and it's all over.

There are many variations on the split-grade printing technique I have described. For example, many fine printers vary the contrast when burning-in areas of a print to give localised control of contrast. Once you have understood the principles involved and seen the impact it can make to your printing, you may well want to experiment with other variations on the theme.

MAKING THE FINAL PRINT

Our test strips have determined the threshold and main exposure and their respective contrast settings. The test strips can be used to assess whether any burning-in or dodging will be necessary and to indicate – in stops – how much additional or reduced exposure will be necessary.

Some photographers prefer to make a 'straight' working print at this stage, knowing that further refinement may be necessary. The advantage is that this print can be annotated with details of exposure and contrast, and the amount of burning and dodging in local areas. This then provides a useful reference print for any subsequent reprinting. Others may prefer to make further test strips to fine-tune exposure information for particularly important areas (such as the sky in a landscape or flesh tones in a portrait).

Whichever approach you prefer, the time will come when, armed with the information you have gathered, you will want to make the full size print. The procedure is as follows:

1) Place our full sheet of paper in the easel and make sure all other details such as focusing and framing are as they were for the test strips.

2) Set the enlarger filtration for grade 0 and expose the paper for the determined basic threshold printing time.

3) Reset the enlarger filtration for the chosen harder grade of paper and expose the paper for the pre-determined main exposure time.

4) Carry out any additional exposure variations to the selected areas (ie dodging and burning-in).

5) Process and dry the print in the normal manner.

6) When dry, we should have a beautiful print which displays a full range of tones from rich deep shadow detail right through to bright sparkling highlights: indeed, a print to be proud of.

Drying is essential as the tonal values of the print change when the print has dried. This is referred to as 'dry down'. Its extent varies between papers, but is far more pronounced on fibre papers than resin-coated papers. Dry down predominantly affects the highlight areas: we can look at a print in the wash dish and see bright sparkling highlight areas, but when dried these may appear dull and degraded.

Provided we remember to dry test strips before making exposure decisions, there is no need to make additional allowance for dry-down. If making exposure decisions from wet test strips (which is not recommended), you may need to make an allowance with fibre based paper of between 7% and 15% of the basic exposure time. (Although natural air-drying is strongly recommended for finished fibre prints, to reduce curl, test strips can be heat dried using a hair dryer or microwave.)

PRINT DRYING

One of the joys of resin coated papers is that they dry flat with very little effort. After washing (for about a minute in running water), gently remove the surface water with a print squeegee and lay the prints on a flat absorbent surface, such as a sheet of blotting paper or card. Prints can be dried quickly using a custom heated print dryer or a hair dryer – after which, leave to cool on a flat surface.

Fibre papers need more careful drying and are prone to curling. There are various techniques to minimise this. Here are a couple of suggestions.

One method is to hang prints back to back on an indoor washing line using plastic clothes pegs. For small sheets of paper (such as 10x8 inches) a clothes peg at each of the four corners is usually sufficient, but larger sheets will benefit from four pegs along top and bottom edges. Allow the prints to dry naturally in a cool, well ventillated dust-free area. The remaining curl (and there will be some!) can be reduced by stacking dried prints, interleaved with sheets of blotting paper, under pressure (such as a pile of books).

Another technique is to carefully sponge off the excess water from the sheet and attach it with masking tape along all four edges to a sheet of plyboard, allowing the paper to dry naturally in a well ventillated dust-free area. Some people recommend pinning the corners.

Whichever technique you use, some edge curl is likely to remain and it is sensible to allow for this when determining your print borders. Having the facility to trim off as little as 1cm along each edge can greatly reduce the problem of flattening the print after drying. This will make mounting the print easier.

If you are fortunate enough to have a heated flat-bed press, then flattening the dried print is a simple matter. There are also heated driers designed for fibre prints, which hold the print against the heated metal with a cloth cover. These can be used in conjunction with glazing plates to achieve high gloss results (assuming you are using glossy paper).

Summary of Lesson 6

- The threshold printing time is the exposure just less than that necessary to register a tone on the paper.

- Printing on grade 0 for the threshold printing time only affects the highlight area of the print.

- Print contrast and tonality in the shadow areas can be controlled by giving the paper a second exposure using a harder grade filtration.

- Split-grade printing techniques offer fine-tuning control over both highlight and shadow areas of the print.

LESSON 7

Presenting your image

This book has concentrated on technical apects of exposure, development and printing. These are the basic tools of the fine photographer's trade, but they are of no value unless the image itself is visually stimulating. And even then, all the hard work that goes into making a fine print can be squandered if the print is not presented attractively. So, in this section of the book, we will focus on:

- Image content and composition
- Print finishing processes, such as toning
- Print presentation

During the previous lessons we have looked at many aspects of the black and white photographic process from a technical point of view. I think you will have gathered by now that I am a strong advocate of good technique. My logic is quite simple: through the mastery of technique we can photograph successfully whatever we wish to photograph.

But good technique is not sufficient to make a good photograph. I have seen prints by several photographers whose technical mastery cannot be questioned but which are, to be candid, as dull as ditchwatcher in the aesthetic sense. It is almost as if they have been more excited by the technical challenges of the subject than by its visual appeal. This is, in my opinion, a sad state of affairs and one I would urge you to avoid.

To make an image, by whatever means, is a creative act: it says something about our relationship to the subject, whether it be delight in natural form, design and beauty, disgust at injustice, empathy with distress, awe of other craft skills, or whatever. This may not be any more refined than "what an attractive face" or "what a beautiful view" – these are perfectly valid artistic statements. The fact that we select a subject to record and present in a photograph means that we feel there is something important about it. To supplement our vital technical skills, we need to consider how we arrange the elements within the picture space and present the print in a way which shows why we thought it was worth recording in the first place. For want of better terms, we might call this 'image appeal' or 'visual impact'.

Image appeal is generated through numerous contributory elements, such as subject interest, impact, emotion, appeal, humour, appreciation or shock. But there is one further important element which binds all these factors together – the composition (or design) of the image. Composition is the arrangement of the elements within an image space.

It is questionable whether composition can be taught. It certainly is not amenable to the sort of rules which can be applied to technical considerations. Composition is generally most effective when it is intuitive: what feels right for a given subject. However, compositional awareness can be heightened by appreciating the work of other artists and by considering some of the techniques which are available for guiding the eye of the viewer or creating tension or harmony within an image. This is a subject about which complete books have been written, so we can only touch here on a few ideas which I have found helpful in thinking about composition.

One piece of simple equipment that I always carry in my pocket is a piece of card with a 6x7cm. aperture cut into it. This is the size of my negative and I use it as my viewing card. Rather than look through the camera's viewfinder I simply hold up the card and move my viewing position around until I find a position which is both visually and compositionally acceptable. Once this position is found I then proceed to set up the camera. I might not always know why one angle 'feels' or works better than another: I trust to instinct.

The compositional 'rule' of which most photographers will have heard is the 'rule of thirds'. This involves splitting the image space, horizontally and vertically, into three equally spaced sections (see figure 16). The intersections of these lines are seen as the strongest points within the picture space and the most important elements are placed at one or more of these intersections.

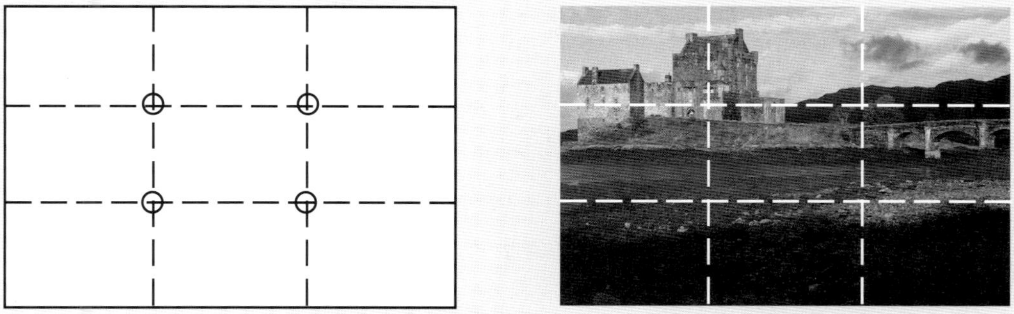

Figure 16 – The 'rule of thirds', although widely dismissed, focuses attention on the arrangement of elements within the picture space, denoting the intersections of third lines as the 'strongest' positions in the image.

It is now fashionable to deride the rule of thirds – and it is widely associated with relatively mindless 'judging' of images in camera club circles. It is, in fact, a corruption of a more complex compositional principle based on observations of natural form. By imitating nature, the 'Golden Mean' was intended to capture in works of art the sense of harmony and perfection of the natural world. Complete dismissal of the 'rule of thirds' is uncharitable: it is a better compositional guideline than 'put your subject in the middle of the picture'. However, any 'rule' of composition has the attendant danger that images will be made to a formula and thus become predictable and boring – literally, thoughtless.

The line (or lines) moving through a picture space will tend to direct the eye. We can use diagonals, curves, s-bends, zigzags, triangles, recession and so on. The list is considerable. Try sketching various shapes within a border representing the area of the print. This helps to heighten compositional awareness and allows you to see what is likely to work. ***Then after all that, remember that there are no 'rules'.***

I would suggest that readers look at both their own work and the work of others to try and analyse why an image works – or why it doesn't. Each of us has the right to put our own interpretation into an image: there is no 'right' and 'wrong' in this area, but awareness of compositional options is vital.

PRINT FINISHING PROCESSES

After all the effort we have put into the creation of our final image the last thing that we need to do is to spoil everything by poor print presentation. It is worthwhile spending a little extra time and effort to ensure that the print is shown to its best advantage. The finishing processes include toning, spotting and mounting.

Personally, I only use two types of toning: selenium and sepia. There are a wide range of other options available, including gold, copper and blue, as well as some systems which allow virtually any colour to be produced. Coloured toning will not make a good image from a dull print: if you want to add colour to your print, make sure that it complements your subject rather than distracting from it.

Selenium toning

As a matter of course, I generally selenium tone fibre based prints, though the intensity of the toning depends on the end result required. Selenium is excellent for archival preservation. I pre-soak the prints to be selenium toned in water at 20°C for approximately 3 minutes before toning.

A dilution of 1:20 for approximately 3 minutes offers archival properties, and gives an extra dimension to the shadow areas. Selenium toner affects the shadow areas of the print far more than the highlights, so always watch the shadow areas for tonal shifts. For archival purposes, remove the print before any colour change takes place.

Conversely, a dramatic colour change takes place if the dilution is reduced to something like 1:6. It is almost impossible to state how long the print should be immersed in the toner because each print and each paper reacts differently. All I can suggest is that you watch the print carefully and as soon as it has acquired the tonality that you require, remove it from the toner and deposit it straight into a tray of cold water.

CAUTION. Care must be taken when using selenium and other toners. Read and follow the manufacturer's instructions. Always use toners in a well ventilated area – you do not need to be in a darkroom. Avoid skin contact by using rubber gloves and/or print tongs. Wearing some form of eye protection is also advisable.

Sepia toning

Most proprietary sepia toners are now based on a thiocarbamide formula, giving the joint benefits of being odourless and offering a variable colour (from yellow to rich dark brown). Sepia is a two-bath process: a bleach followed (after careful washing) by the toner. It also adds to the archival permanence of the print.

The finished colour effect will depend on the paper and developer used, the strength and extent of bleaching, the length of toning and the mix of the toning solution. You can chose a very subtle effect or rich colour, depending on what suits the mood you want to create in the image. I suggest you start by following the manufacturer's processing recommendations and vary these, if necessary, in the light of experience. As always, observe the health and safety instructions provided by the manufacturer.

PRINT PRESENTATION

The first thing I do when viewing the print for the first time after it has dried is to take two white L-shaped cards that I have made and place these on the borders of the print. Doing this lets me see the image with a frame around it. I then move the cards around the picture to judge whether the print contains extraneous detail that does not enhance the end result. If this is the case then I will measure the dimensions of the aperture which shows the print off to its best advantage and know what size to make the aperture in the print overlay.

The next step is to examine for print imperfections. These normally appear in the form of little white spots which appear (however carefully the negative is cleaned before exposure) from dust which has settled on the negative during printing. We have to accept this and learn how to remove these spots from our prints.

This action is known as Spotting. Spotting is yet another little skill that we need to be able to perform in order that we may present our prints properly. Many fine art photographers use Spotone dyes, which come in six shades and which can be mixed to match the tone of the paper. The other requirements are a spotting brush (the best ones to use are sable hair size 00 or 0) and an old flat dish or saucer.

Put a tiny amount of each dye around the top edge of the dish and allow this to dry. When you are ready to start spotting, use the brush almost dry or just moist. Put the tip of the brush into the selected colour (or mix a combination of the colours) just sufficiently to pick up some dye. Before committing to the finished print, try the colour match or the reaction firstly on either an old print or the white border of the print to be spotted. When satisfied that everything is okay, gently touch the spot with the tip of the brush. Don't worry if you don't cover the offending spot in one go, after a couple of dabs leave the dye to dry (it only takes a minute or two) and then go back and dab on a little more until eventually the spot disappears.

There are alternative spotting media. One which has gained in popularity recently is the SpotPen system (distributed in Europe by Tetenal) and I have now been converted to this system personally. SpotPens look like fine felt tip pens, but contain spotting dyes in a range of shades of grey (neutral and warmtone versions are available). They are relatively expensive, but many photographers find them a more convenient way of spotting.

When the spotting is complete, it is time to conduct the final acts of mounting and overlaying the print. The methods I use are as follows:

Mounting

To mount the print on backing board I now use the self adhesive mounting board produced by Daler Studland. This is fairly expensive, but it does allow the print to lie perfectly flat, is very easy to use, and does not require any special skills or equipment. It only takes a minute or so to apply and is available from art shops.

In the past I have used dry mounting, adhesive spray and hinge mounting. Of these the best is dry mounting, without doubt, but you still need to purchase very smooth backing board otherwise the texture shows up through the print. It is a matter of finding the method which best suits you.

Overlays

I feel that prints are shown to their best advantage when surrounded by a mitred, off-white or antique white overlay. Some people prefer mid-grey or even black ones. However, I feel that the softness of the white is more appealing.

If I am going to frame the print, then I prefer a very narrow black frame, though I also like slightly wider wooden frames. Again it is down to personal preferences, but do look for mounts and frames that complement rather than compete with your photographs.

To cut the overlay, I first determine the size of the aperture to be cut by using L shaped cards as described earlier. I then use a rotary cutter to cut the overlay to the outside dimensions required.

On the back of the overlay, I draw faint centre lines with a pencil. I then mark the size of the aperture required by using the centre lines, and proceed to cut with an angled (45°) mat cutter, making doubly sure that the cutting blade is pointing towards the outside edge of the overlay. Cuts should be made using several light cuts rather than trying to achieve the cut in one pass. Attempting to cut through the overlay in one pass more often than not leads to damage. Take the cutting edge slightly beyond the corners of the aperture so that the off-cut drops out freely and does not damage the internal corners. Following this I dress up the cut edges by rubbing lightly with a small emery board (as used by ladies for filing their finger nails).

I place several small pieces of double sided sticky tape on the very outside edge or white borders of the print and proceed very careful to align my print. Once I am satisfied with the alignment, I present the overlay to the print and press lightly down. Job completed. We now have a first class photograph presented in a first class and professional manner.

If you have not mounted the print, you will need to turn over the matted print and secure each edge of the print to the mat with masking tape.

Summary of Lesson 7

This lesson has dealt with:

- The importance of image content and composition.
- The use of selenium and sepia toners.
- Spotting the print.
- Mounting the print and cutting mitred overlays.

LESSON 8

Examples

This book places the emphasis on technical understanding to achieve fine quality in monochrome printing. However, these skills are just the tools to help you get your pre-visualised image on paper. What counts at the end of the day is the visual appeal of the image produced. With that in mind, I thought it would be appropriate to conclude these lessons by looking at some of my own prints – time to stand up and be counted!

These images are not in any way intended to be examples of what you should be trying to achieve, nor are they supposed to be some model of perfection to aspire to. They are merely vehicles for relating the theory and principles we have discussed in the book to the practice of making photographs. I will write a little about the challenges which each presented and the methods used.

I have included a number of photographs, most of which were taken a good while ago. They have been selected for no better reasons than that they are reasonably varied and the negatives were not too difficult to find!

All of the originals were printed on fibre based paper, but have been printed again on Ilford resin coated paper for reproduction purposes.

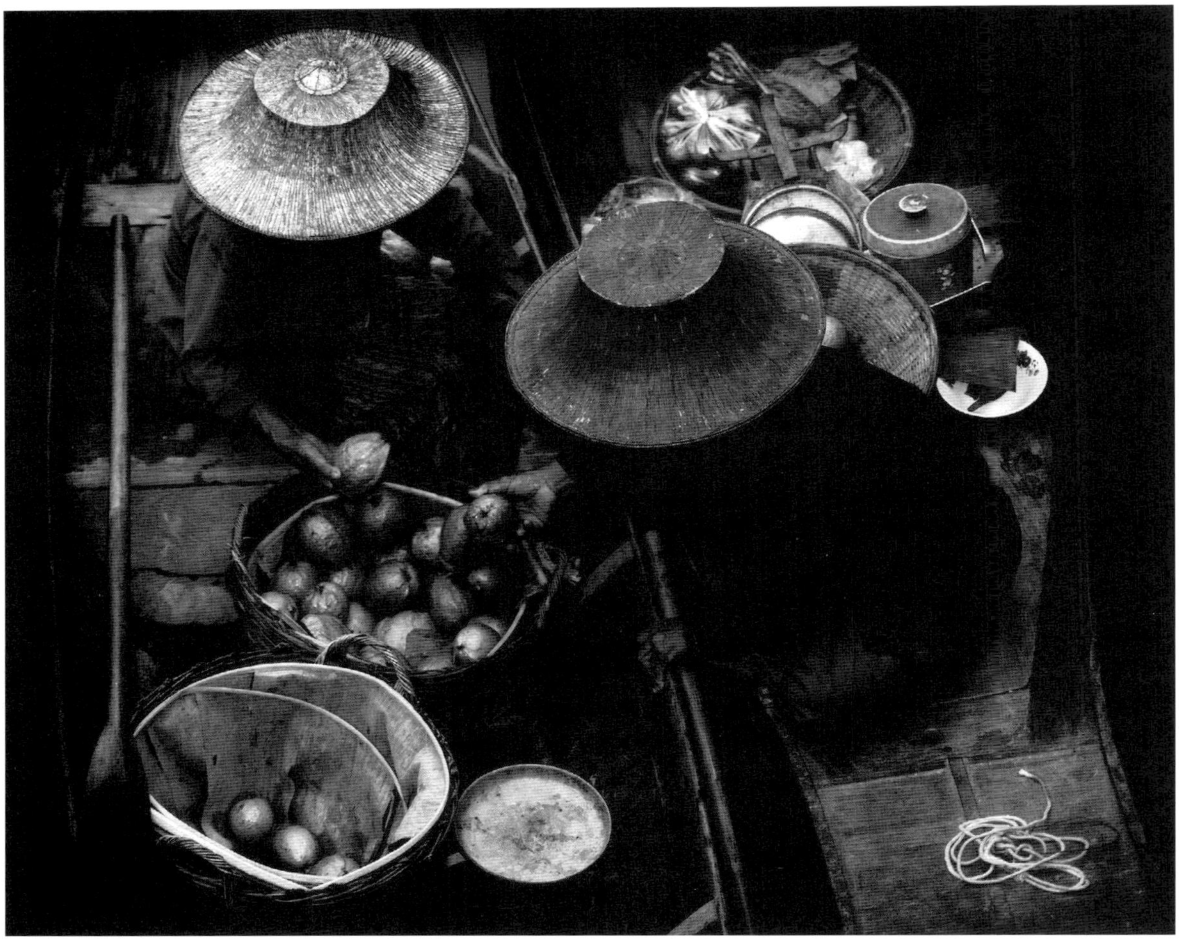

Thai Traders

This was one of my earliest pictures produced by using the Zone System and is still one of my personal favourites. The photograph was taken in very poor lighting conditions. It was the back end of the monsoon period and it had been pouring with rain only a few minutes before. At the time, I had only learnt about exposing the film correctly and had not started increasing or decreasing development times according to the subject contrast.

I took a spot meter reading from the dark part of the jacket worn by the woman on the right and closed down my lens by two stops from the indicated exposure (ie placing this shadow value on Zone III).

With the benefit of hindsight and my current experience, I would now place that area of the jacket on Zone II (which would necessitate closing down by three stops). I would also have metered from the white saucer and determined my development time by considering this as Zone VIII (indicating N+2 development time to allow for the low contrast of the scene). As I had unwittingly under-developed the film by two stops, I ended up with one of the thinnest negatives I have had to print from. The final print was produced on Ilford Multigrade FB using enlarger filtration to give paper grade 4.5. It is a straight print except for a little burning-in to darken the reflections from the water at the right and left sides of the boats (+1 stop) and also at the top and bottom edges (+0.5 stop).
Camera: Bronica ETRS; 150mm Lens. Film: Ilford FP4 Rated at ISO 50.

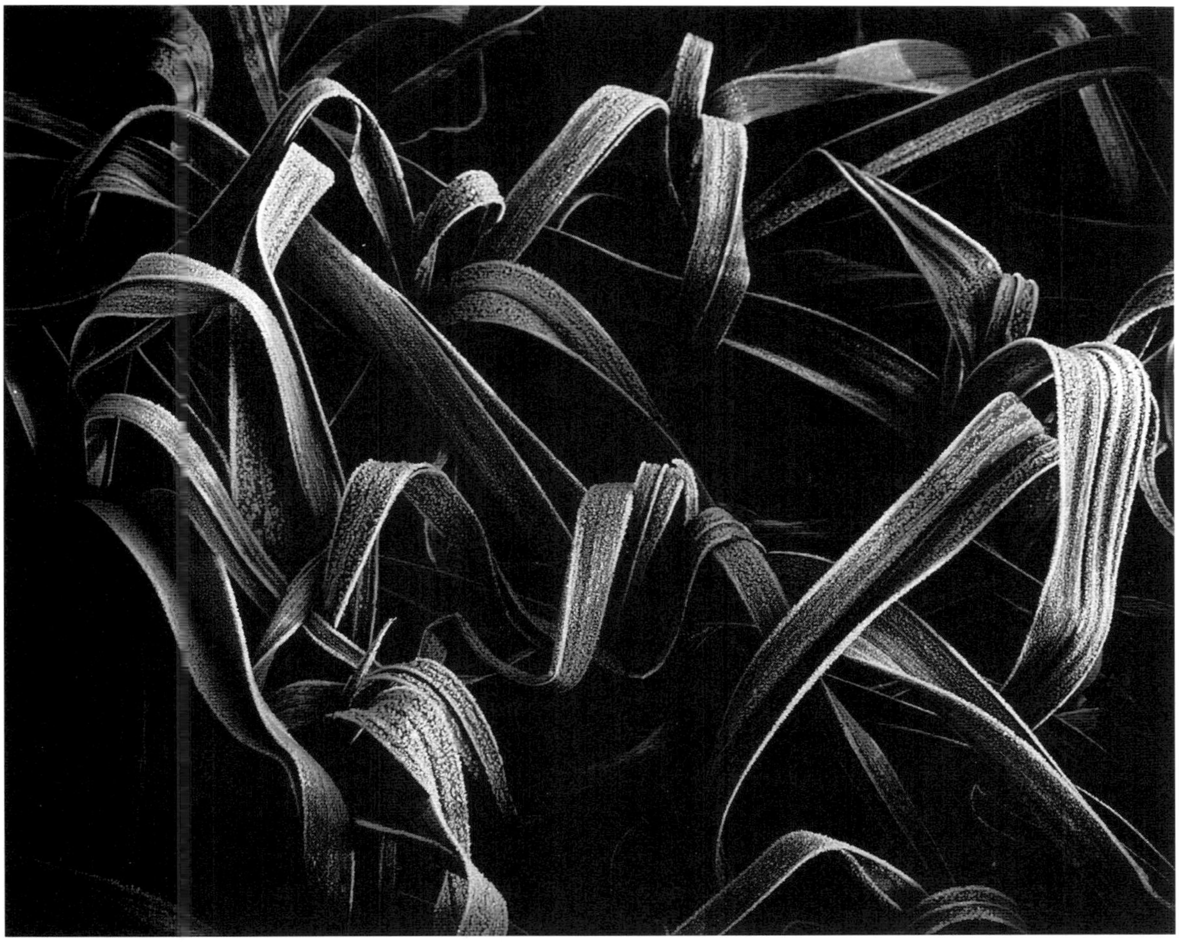

Leeks

This has been included for no other reason than its simplicity. I do suffer withdrawal symptoms if I have not taken a photograph for a few days and was beginning to feel really fed up because I had not been out. I picked up my camera bag and on a cold and frosty morning wandered down to the local allotments. I was intrigued by the shapes formed by the frost on the leek leaves.

Again, this was during my early Zone System days before adjusting development times for subject contrast range. I metered for the fully textured frost and placed this on Zone VII by opening up two stops from that indicated by my meter. The soil actually only fell on Zone IV (a four stop tonal range). If I had known then what I know now, I would have placed the soil on Zone III and increased development to N+1, to put more contrast in the negative. I think this period was the dawning of my awareness that images could be created from almost nothing, provided that the photographer was in control.

The original is a straight print on Ilford Multigrade FB grade 4. All the edges were burnt in by +0.75 stop to help keep the viewers' attention towards the central area of the print.

Camera: Bronica ETRS; 150mm lens plus No.1 close up filter. Film: Agfa APX, rated at ISO 50.

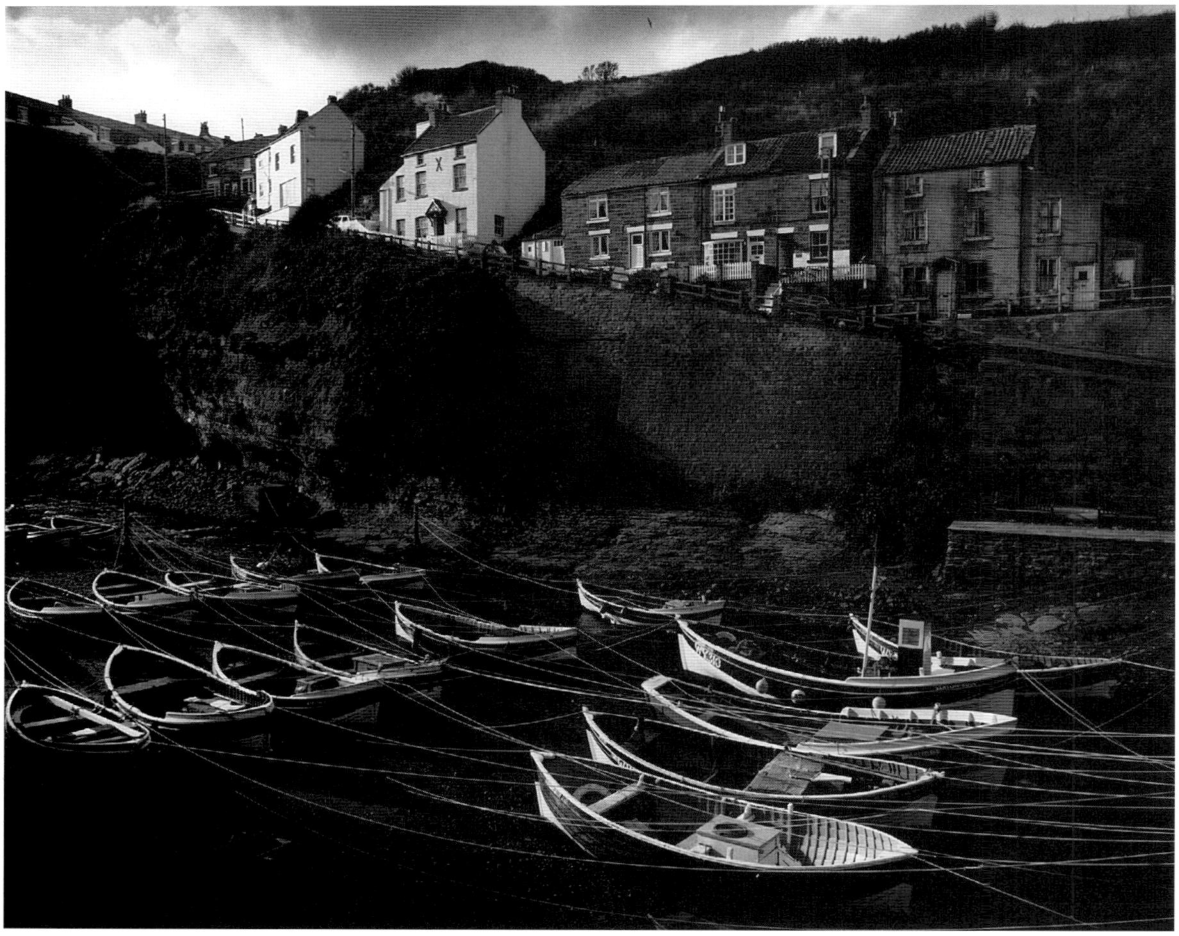

Staiths

By the time I took this photograph, I had been using the Zone System for a couple of years and felt totally confident using the system for the subject exposure. Although I was increasing development times, I was still not developing the film as fully as I am today. I knew that my printing had improved by leaps and bounds through the benefit of having good negatives, but in reality I was in those days not fully in control of the printing.

The skill of producing a quality print was still a little hit and miss for me. I saw some work by American Master Printer George Tice. One of his prints was at Staiths and I wondered if I could produce a print anywhere near as good as his. Well, I think my original print on Agfa Record Rapid grade 4 paper is not too far away from his, but I bet he printed his a lot easier and quicker than I did. I sweated for a full evening on this one! This print today causes me no problems whatsoever, so I guess that I must have improved a little since then.

The original print on Agfa Record Rapid was developed in Agfa Neutol WA developer to produce nice warm tones. It is a straight print other than burning-in the sky (+2 stops), the bottom of the print (+1 stop), and the sides for (+0.5 stop each).

Camera: Bronica ETRS, 80mm lens. Film: Agfa APX rated at ISO 50.

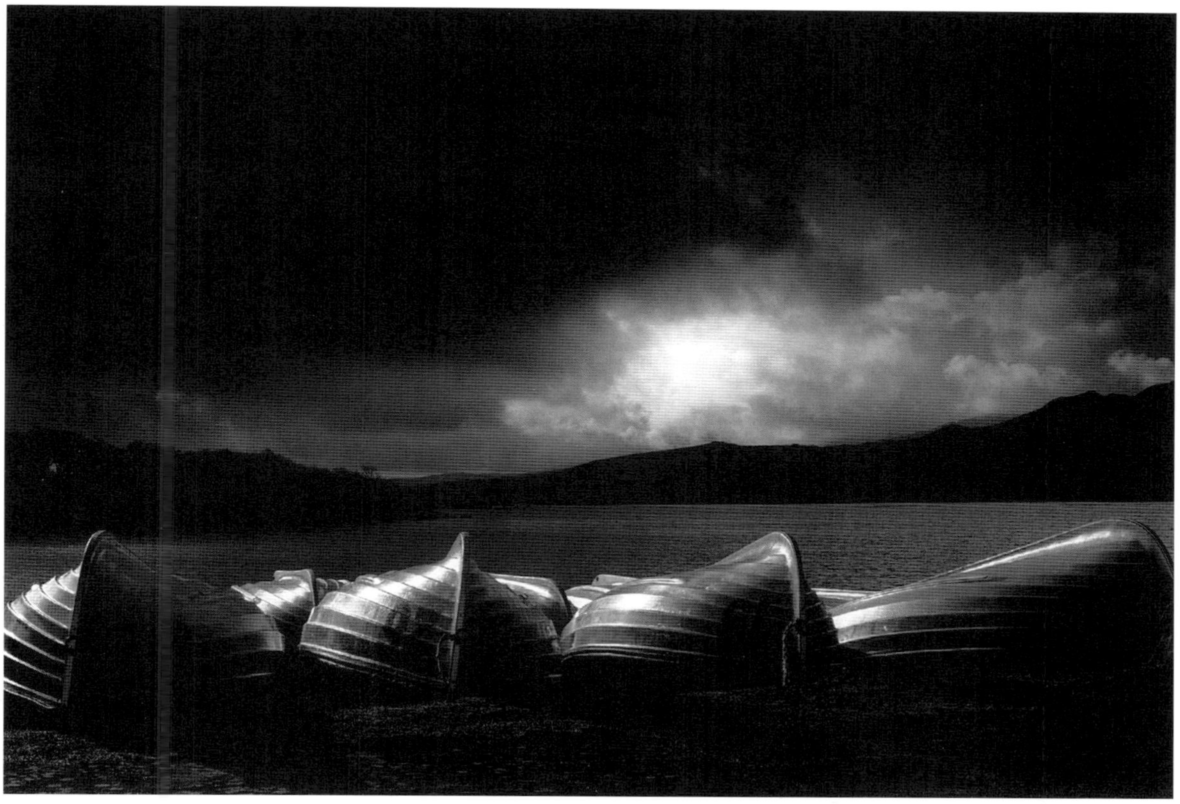

When the visitors are gone

I've included this photograph because of its drama. It was a foul cold November morning; the sky was black, when suddenly the edge of a storm cloud came into sight. I quickly set up the camera. I metered from the highlight on the boats and wished for these to fall on Zone VIII, so I opened up the lens by three stops compared to the reading given by my exposure meter. The highlight in the sky was not quite as bright as the one on the boats so I knew that there would be no problem with containing the sky detail at around Zone VII. The detail on the shadow side of the boat fell on Zone II, so again I knew that this would reproduce as a shadow area containing just discernible detail – exactly what I wanted.

The original print was produced on Ilford Multigrade FB paper on grade 2.5. I was happy to have the neutral to cool tones of this paper considering the weather conditions. The highlight area on the sky was dodged for -0.75 stop during base exposure. The rest of the sky was given +2.5 stops exposure to bring in the drama of the storm clouds.

Using more up to date techniques, this print is a prime candidate for split-grade printing: find the threshold printing time on grade 0 for the sky highlight, then print the secondary exposure at grade 4, again dodging the sky highlight for -0.75 stop to prevent exceeding the highlight threshold. Then burn-in the rest of the sky for +2.5 stops.

Camera: Linhof 6x7, 80mm lens; film: Ilford FP4 Plus Rated at ISO 50.
N (Normal) Development.

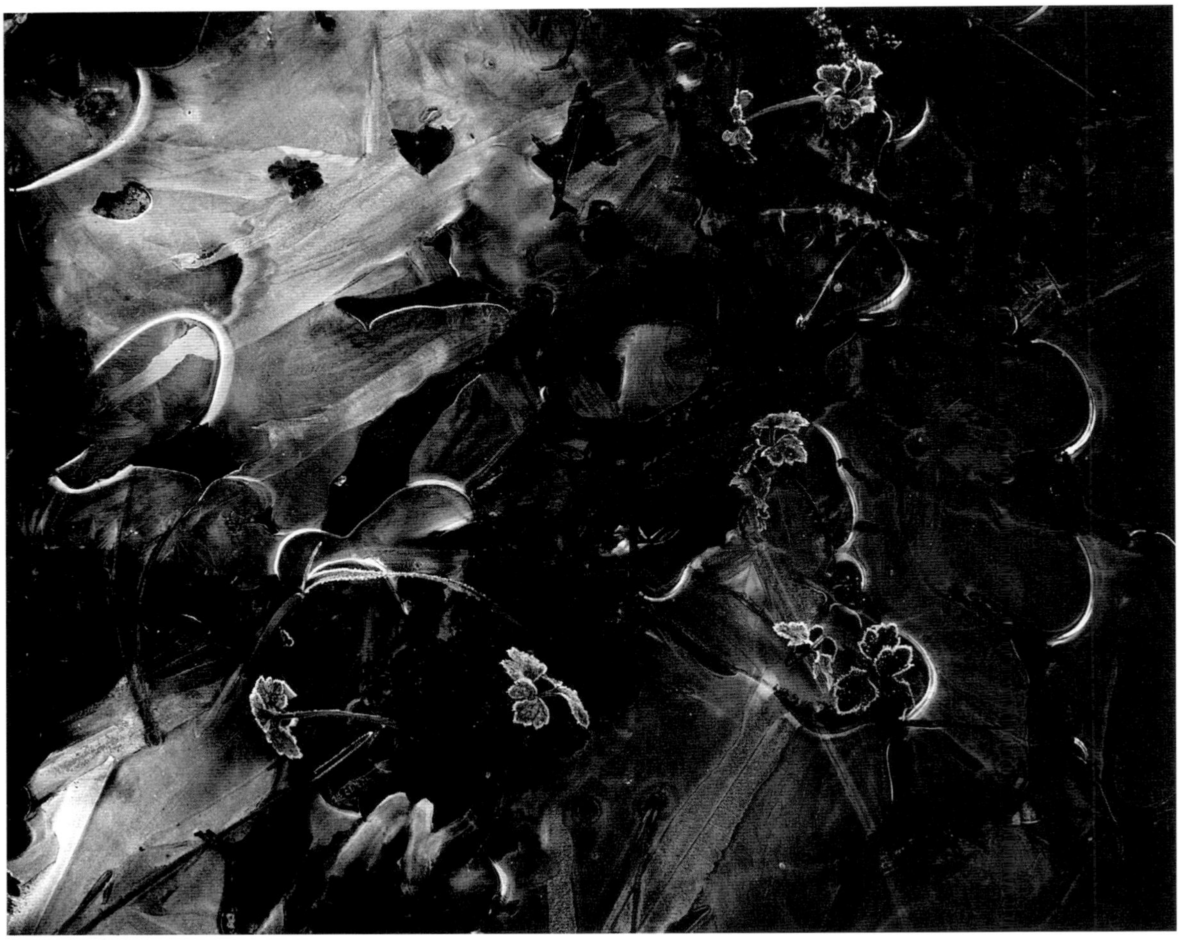

Frost pool and leaves

I love abstract images and feel that we need to develop a different 'seeing eye' in order to take this type of photograph. Instead of looking at the grand vista, we need to move in closer and become accustomed to looking for detail that looks aesthetically interesting (generally in the shape or form).

The tonal range of the subject matter was just over three stops. I gave the film N+1 development to push the ice in the top left hand corner up to Zone VI. The highlights on the leaves and ice bubbles are then nicely controlled.

The original is a straight print on Ilford Multigrade FB, grade 4. All the four edges of the print having been given +0.5 stop burning-in to contain the image. This negative will print readily onto paper grades 2 or 3, but I preferred the choice of grade 4.

Camera: Linhof 6x7, 80mm lens; film: Ilford FP4 Plus rated at ISO 50.

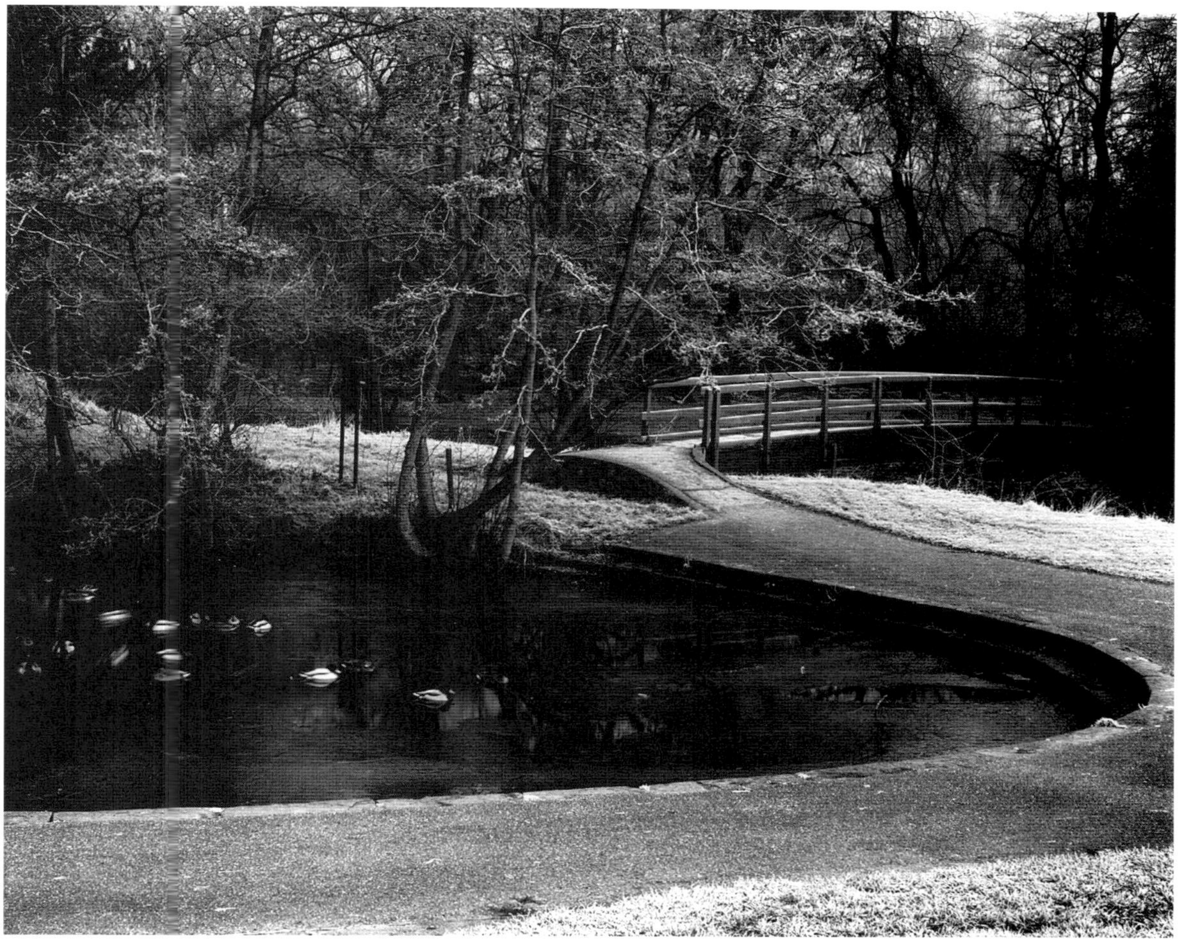

Bramhall Park

This was made early one bitterly cold December morning between Christmas and New Year. I was out very early to avoid the inevitable number of people who would soon be out walking in the park. I liked the curve of the footpath leading to the footbridge, the line of which had been enhanced by the frost. I also felt that a degree of intrigue existed caused mainly by the darkness looming on the far side of the bridge.

The contrast range was only three stops. I metered for the frost and put this on Zone VII and let the lower value tonal areas fall to their natural Zone. I knew before firing the camera shutter that this photograph would need to be printed on Grade 4. My exposure meter told me that I needed to expose this scene for 1 second. I therefore gave it 2 seconds to allow for reciprocity failure.

The original print is on Ilford Multigrade FB, grade 4. It is a straight print with +0.3 stop burn-in along all four edges.

Camera: Linhof 6x7, 80mm lens; film: Ilford FP4 Plus rated at ISO 50.

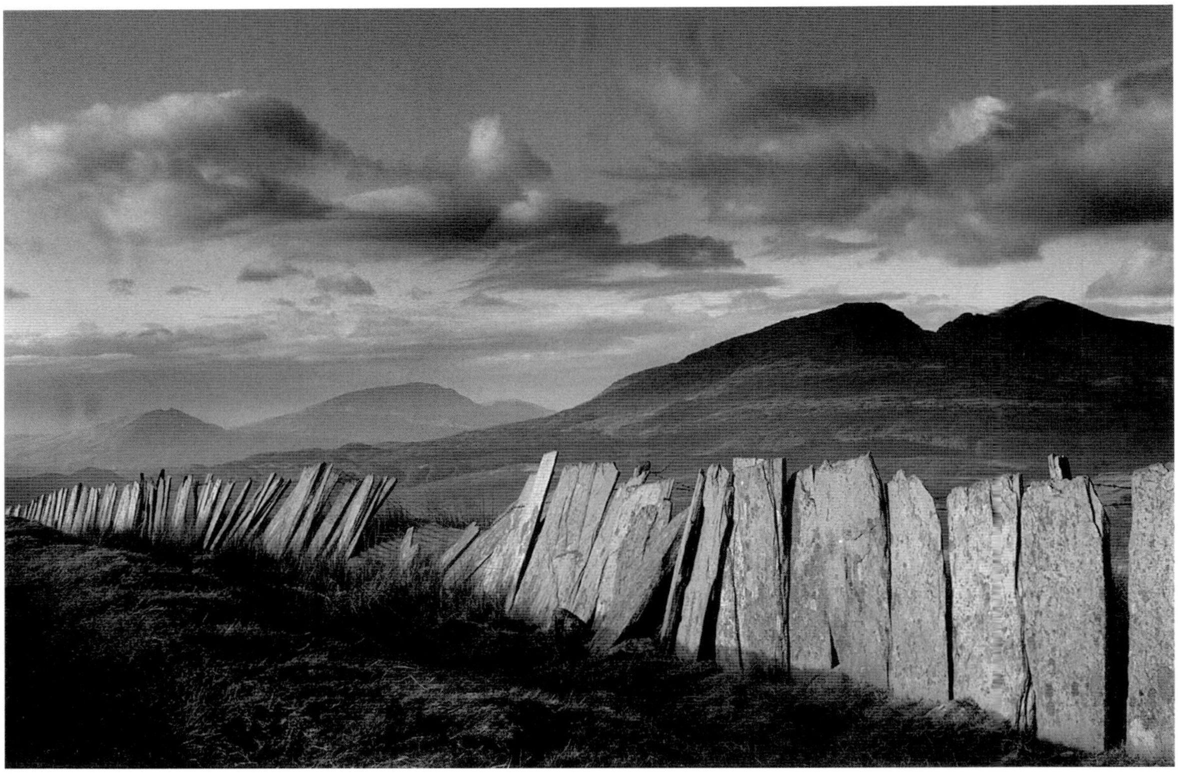

Slate fence

A very gentle, easy on the eye, landscape. I metered the fully textured shadow area (this was in the grass which fell into heavy shadow) and placed this on Zone III. I found that the strongest highlight on the slate fence fell on Zone VII. This is what I wanted: a fully textured highlight showing on the fence. The remainder of the fence fell onto a high Zone VI which is what I visualised. The contrast range of the scene was just about right, showing a five stop range between Zone III and Zone VII. No filters were used. Normal (N) development was given to the film.

The original print was produced on Agfa Multicontrast Classic FB grade 3. Developed in Ilford PQ Universal. Straight print with the bottom left hand corner being given 0.75 stop extra exposure and the sky being given + 2 stops.
Camera: Linhof 6x7, 80mm lens; film: Ilford FP4 Plus rated at ISO 50.

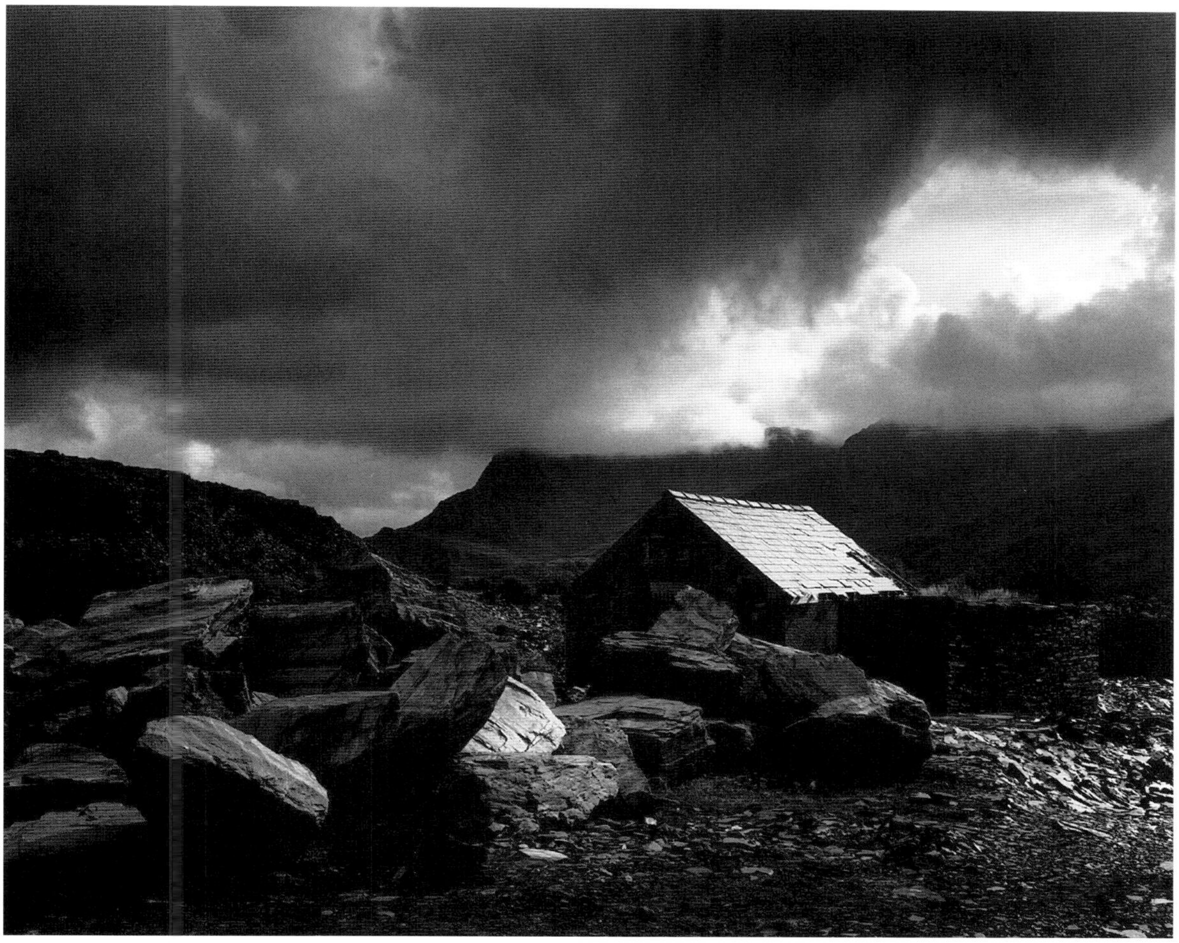

Slate quarry, Nantlle

The drama of North Wales is typified in this photograph, not only because of its natural beauty, but also because of man's intrusion. I often visit the slate quarries and would defy anyone remotely interested in photography not to take photographs, such is the power of appeal.

When I came across this scene, the clouds were scudding across the sky causing the light to change rapidly. For fear of missing the shot, I jumped out of the car and used the camera hand-held. I quickly metered the scene: the tonal range was good, displaying a range from Zone II (just discernible shadow detail) on the underside of the large rocks to Zone VIII (just discernible highlight detail) on the edge of the clouds.

The original print was made on Ilford Multigrade FB, split-graded by printing to highlight threshold on grade 0 and then giving a secondary exposure on grade 4 to bring in the print contrast. The sky was given +2 stops exposure and the bottom left corner (up to the first boulder showing highlight detail) and the bottom right corner were both given +1 stop extra exposure on Grade 4 to stop the highlights from pulling the viewer's eye away from the focal point of the picture. *Camera: Mamiya 7, 65mm Lens. Film: Kodak T-Max 400 developed in Ilford ID11.*

Epilogue

If you remember nothing else from this book, keep hold of the fact that the secret of the Zone System is to meter from the shadows and then close down the lens by two stops. Once you have mastered that, then all you need to do is get your development times sorted out.

Enjoy taking photographs and keep it simple so as not to confuse yourself. I cannot think of one advantage that working in a complicated manner offers, so why not go for go for simplicity and good sound technique? I feel confident that you will reap the rewards.

I believe this book has covered everything from a technical perspective that is needed to make superb monochrome prints. The point of sound technique is not to constrain or limit your photography, but to free your creativity and enable you to express your feelings for a subject more successfully by taking control of the process. All that's left now is to pick up your camera gear and go out and shoot some film.

Good shooting.

Index

Adams, Ansel	7, 34
Burning-in	34
Characteristic curve	9, 32
Closing down	14, 15
Composition	48-50
Contrast	25-29
D-Max	11, 32
Depth of field	15
Dodging	33
Dry-down	46
Exposure Index	14
Exposure meter	17
Exposure stops	14
Exposure Value	16
F-Stop printing	37
F-Stop ready reckoner	40
Fibre-based paper	30-31
Film	9
Film base + fog	9, 32
Film speed	13
Film-developer combination	25
Golden Zones	18, 28
Grain	13
Grey card	16
High key	21
Ilford ID11	25
Ilford Multigrade IV	31
ISO speed	23
Latent image	9
Light meter	15, 16
Low key	21
Max black	11, 32-33
Mounting	51
Multigrade paper	*see Variable contrast paper*
N+ and N- development	27-28
Negative density	9, 11
Nocon, Gene	37
Normal development time	25, 27
Opening up	14, 15
Overlays	51-52
Paper	30-33
Paper base white	10, 32
Paper developers	34-35
Paper grades	31, 40
Personal development times	24-25
PQ Universal	35
Pre-flashing	34
Pre-visualisation	7
Print density	11
Print drying	47
Print finishing	50
Print map	41
Print presentation	51-52
Print tongs	42
Resin coated paper	30-31
Rule of thirds	49
Selenium toning	50
Sepia toning	50
Silver halides	9
Split-grade printing	45-46
Spot meter	17
Spotting	35, 51
Test strips	37-39
Textured Zones	20
Threshold printing	44-45
Tice, George	56
Tonal values	18
Tripod	13
Variable contrast paper	30-31
Visual impact	48
Zone System	7 et seq
– advantages	8

CREATIVE IMAGE WORKSHOPS

For those wanting personal tuition, Harry Fearn runs a workshop centre offering a wide range of courses. These include the Zone System and F-Stop printing, as well as special guest photographer programmes. The workshops cater for individuals, small groups, camera clubs and Educational Authority tuition for both tutors and pupils. Further information is available from: The Creative Image, Snowdon Mill, Porthmadog, North Wales, LL49 9DF. Tel: (UK code) 01766 513853.

THE CREATIVE MONOCHROME EXPERIENCE

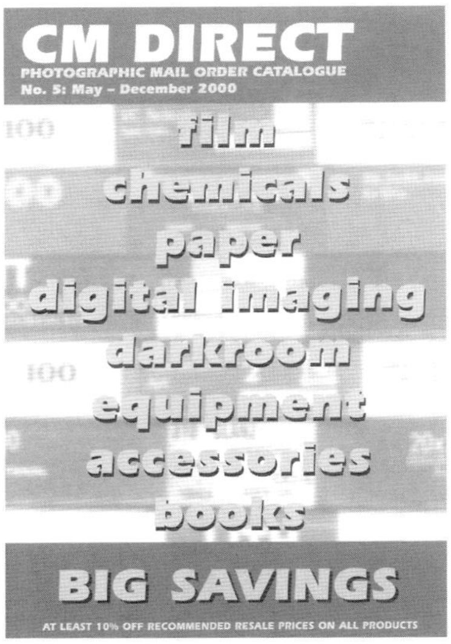

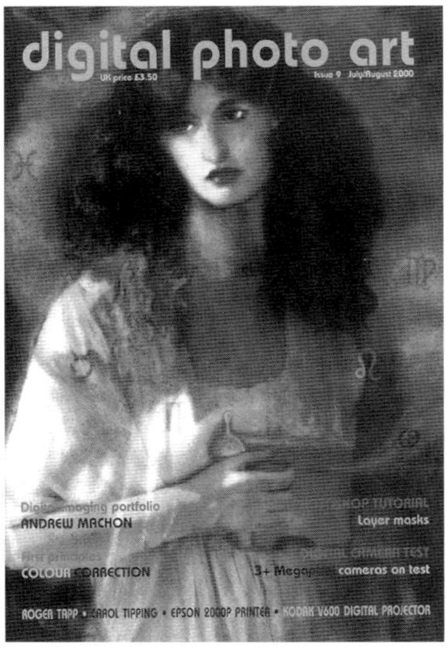

Creative Monochrome – the publisher of this book – exists to further the art and craft of photography in all its forms. Our brief is to enthuse, inform and inspire photographers. We seek to achieve this by publishing books and magazines, and by providing a mail order service for photographic equipment and materials.

Monochrome is a particular passion. We run a group for enthusiasts, whatever their level of experience – Friends of Creative Monochrome has around 5,000 members worldwide. Friends receive our bi-monthly magazine Mono, the CM Direct catalogue and a wide range of special offers and discounts. We also invite Friends to enter prints for our yearbook of members' work, Best of Friends, which normally contains around 150 prints by more than 100 different photographers.

Membership of Friends of Creative Monochrome costs just £8.50 per year and is open to all.

To join the Friends of Creative Monochrome and to receive details of our other publications and our CM Direct catalogue, write to: Creative Monochrome Limited, Courtney House, 62 Jarvis Road, South Croydon, Surrey, CR2 6HU. Tel: 020 8686 3282 or fax: 020 8681 0662.

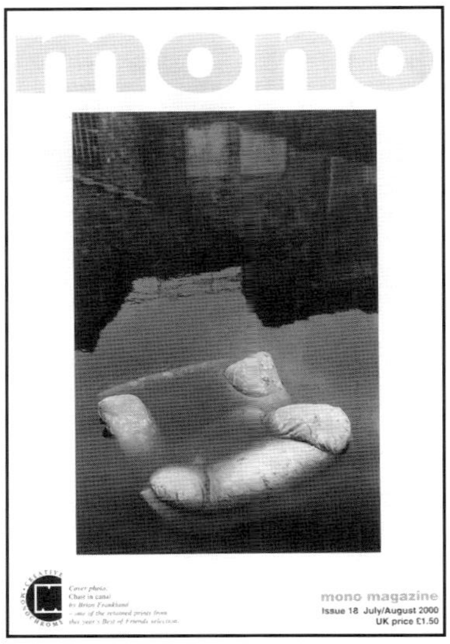

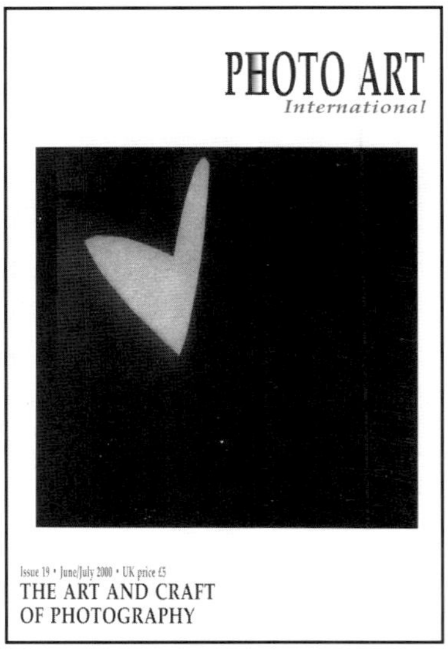